ORDINARY LIVES

edited by
CLIVE MURPHY

A Pimlico basement. An invalid, with the simplicity of illness, dreams of his fabulous past and pipe-dreams as fabulous a future. His wife, Johanna, sustains this eager listener with herring, hearing sandwiches...

I offer Four Acres and a Donkey, *the third volume and the inspiration of my series 'Ordinary Lives' to my friend Johanna, now a widow.*

EDITOR

FOUR ACRES AND A DONKEY

S. A. B. Rogers

FOUR ACRES
AND A DONKEY

Recorded during August and September, 1970

LONDON : DENNIS DOBSON

I dedicate this book
to
my beloved mother
who
rests in her grave among
the windswept hills of Derbyshire

First published in Great Britain 1979 by
Dobson Books Ltd, 80 Kensington Church Street, London, W8

Printed in Great Britain by
Bristol Typsetting Co, Ltd,
Barton Manor, St Philips, Bristol

ISBN 0 234 72066 2

CONTENTS

The Accident

One night early in 1969 I went into Leicester Square Toilet at a quarter to ten. I washed the kettle out and put it on the stove and while I was drawing water to fill the kettle I saw a pair of feet on the floor behind a door. 'A dosser,' I thought. 'I'll leave him there. He's a meths drinker.' These meths drinkers, if you try to get them up, sometimes hit you with a bottle—a big cider bottle or a wine bottle. I didn't want no stitches in my head so I left him for a few hours to cool off.

At a quarter past eleven two policemen walked down. They come to my office and said, 'Rodge, you've got a dosser here!' I said, 'Yes, I know. He's been here since quarter to ten. Would you like a drink of tea, constables?' They said, 'No thanks, but we'll have this dosser out.' 'Well,' I said, 'I was thinking of leaving him till one o'clock till I clean up. He may have slept it off by then. If you disturb these people they throw the bottle at you. They're usually mental.' They said, 'We'll have him out *now*!'

I got the ladder. I couldn't open the door. He was a big man with a big pair of boots on and I was going to climb over the top to get inside to pull his feet up for the police to arrest him. I put the ladder against the door and when I climbed to the top it slipped on the tiles and I hit the cover of the man-hole to the sewers. I weighed sixteen stone eight and I hit it so hard I saw the loveliest green flash I ever saw in my life. I broke my glasses. My singlet was spattered with blood. The policemen run into my cabin and grabbed towel after towel, then they radioed for the ambulance.

9

Next a CID man was down with the news that a man across the road at the Empire Theatre, Mr Marshall, had just been robbed of a thousand pounds. A car drew up, a small Mini with three men in, two got out and the driver kept the engine going, and Mr Marshall was coming out with two leather bags and five hundred pounds in each bag to put in the all-night safe and they clobbered him on the head.

My ambulance was in front and we was both taken to Charing Cross Hospital. Mr Marshall, he needed fourteen stitches. I heard him groaning. He was behind the next curtain to me. He was unconscious for three days. I had four stitches put in the side of my head and I was back at work the next day with a big plaster on and after six weeks the Council sent me a ten pound cheque to get a pair of glasses.

But soon I found I couldn't walk properly, couldn't run and couldn't go upstairs on a bus to smoke my pipe. I found out my speed was slowering and slowering and slowering. I went to the doctor. He said, 'I think it's only your bronchitis but I'll put you into Westminster Hospital just in case.' I lay in Erskine Ward thinking it all over. 'What shall I do—give up the job or go back to work earning?' They didn't tell me in the hospital I'd brain damage and heart failure as well as my bronchitis—my doctor told me when I come out. So I retired and my doctor, he's been a friend to me ever since. He's a marvellous doctor. He's a full surgery every night. He's worked to death. My wife, Johanna, goes round and gets the prescriptions off his secretary. He gives me energy tablets, brain tablets, bronchitis tablets, penicillin tablets, tablets for the bladder and Tuinal tablets to slow the heart-beat down and make me sleep. I take about a hundred and ten tablets a week. I'm like a slot machine, a parking meter. My wife now puts the Tuinal in a cupboard in the lounge and carries the key with her and when I want a tablet I've got to ask her.

The penicillin and the Tuinal are in plastic, the shape of a bullet. I twist them round, break them in half and pour the contents out into a dessert spoon and then I dip the spoon into fresh cold water, shake it a little bit and drink the powder off the spoon. You're supposed to take these tablets whole, plastic and all, but I've thrown one or two in the sink and they stick there and you can't pull them off and when you try they stretch like elastic. So I throw the plastic away, I don't fancy *that* in my inside. One morning I got up at four and had a Tuinal. I broke it into halves, put it in a spoon and dipped it in my mug of water. My wife got up when I'd gone back to bed and took a drink and went fast asleep for two hours. Two of these tablets will put the strongest man to sleep in ten minutes. I can take eight a day and stay awake if I want to. If you saw me when I've had them you'd think I was drunk.

I usually get up at five o'clock in the dark and put on my dressing-gown and let the dogs out and go to the toilet. The toilet's in the back yard. In front of where you sit down there's a big bill about two feet square and on it's the Lord's Prayer. Then on one of the walls I've got the Mona Lisa. On the other wall I've got Clint Eastwood in *Gunsmoke* with his big .38 Colt stuck out and his silver watch and chain. A young boy about twenty years of age give it to me in Piccadilly Toilet. He said, 'There's a carve-out for you, Rodge.' I said 'Thank you very much.'

I go to the toilet the Indian way. I don't use coggage. When I come inside I wash my bum and light a joss stick and put it in front of my Buddha in the lounge to make the room smell nice and I say a prayer. The prayer comes from my heart, not from the head : 'Give all and receive nothing. Build, do not destroy.'

I drink a glass of water for breakfast and then I smoke my pipe and read the *Telegraph*—the births and marriages and deaths and wrestling and swimming and what the Queen's doing and who she's entertaining. At ten I take a sleeping tablet and go back to bed till about twelve. Then I sit and think with the dogs and cat round me till dinner. Then I take another sleeping tablet to knock me out till 'Crossroads' on the television at 4.30 and after supper I smoke my pipe and go on watching television till about nine. I watch Westerns, 'Stars on Sunday', wrestling, ballet ... When I was working in Covent Garden Toilets by St Paul's Old Church in the market I tried to get a ticket to the Russian Ballet but they were all sold. On nights I saw people coming in lovely cars and limousines and they'd park them all round the toilets, all round the market. Ladies had their finery on and the men were in evening dress. I'd like to sit amongst these people and see a Russian ballet or an English ballet. When I watch ballet on television I'm not ashamed to say I take my glasses off and I cry. Ballet touches me. It's so beautiful to see these ladies on their toes and the music going with them and the rhythm. It's something out of this world. Rudolf Nureyev is a marvel. When he glides through the air he gets women sobbing, he gets me sobbing. He's not only a great dancer, he's a great lover. I can see that. It's the build of the man and he's got youth on his side. Any man that's travelled the world would know in a second that Rudolf Nureyev was a great lover. I study nature.

I've only been out once in about seven months because when I walk about three hundred yards I've got to stop and get my breath. I'm a heavy built man. It's all very well the doctor saying, go on a diet and eat lettuce and do this and that, but he's not married to a German woman who cooks hot meals. What I'd like to do one night is go out to a nice clean pub or a hotel like the Dorchester and have one glass of beer and come home again. But I'm really a home bird. I'm a poor one at making friends. I don't dislike people. I like conversation but I like *sensible* conversation. Sometimes we've had people in the lounge and they've spoke to me and I've been bored in ten minutes. Once I fell asleep and the next morning I said to my wife, 'By God, I don't want that again! They just sat and talked about Yorkshire. I've seen better places than Yorkshire!'

I'm cosmopolitan. I like to talk about everything. I like to meet a man and try my brains against his. I like a good argument. In Manchester I used to speak at Queen's Park Parliament Hut. Twice a week I was on a platform at a green baize table with what they call a 'carafe' full of cold water and a glass and we used to have debates. It was a big army hut and was packed to the door and we debated on Politics, Economics, Sociology, Psychology, Entymology, Biology. I used to mostly speak about Eastern Languages and how they live in the East and how they drink and sleep in the East on the charpoys and the foods they like and how they won't eat bacon and eggs. I used to lecture to them. I was getting on for about twenty-six and I'd a big blackboard with my name on, 'Brahma Will Speak On So and So' and people used to question me. It wasn't a case of winning the argument. I used to have a debate with the people. That's what I like. But when you get somebody come down here to see me from outside and they don't know anything, only about their work and they don't even know much about their work, well you can't get much conversation out of a person who talks about Mrs So and So and Mr So and So and the weather. It's mostly gossip and I leave that to the old ladies.

One of the dustbin men that comes down to empty our dustbins, I know him personally. He and a few others used to come down to Piccadilly every morning half past seven prompt, bar Saturday and Sunday. They'd say, 'Hello, Rodge. Have you got the key?' I'd say 'Yes. Here you are. I'll go through the washroom and open the door for you,' and they used to empty about eight dustbins into big red sacks and one used to lift them on the other's back and they had to carry them all through the toilets out up the stairs out into the street.

Being a dustbin man's a heavy job. They only last ten years. Then they're broken men, finished.

I've had some of them in here for cups of tea. The Depot's only across the way in Gatliff Road. When I'm sat here on my own in the morning I can hear them. They tap on the window to me. I say, 'Hello there! Hello! Wait a minute!' and I run out and open the door and go out in front and talk to them. I say, 'How's the Dilly now?' 'Oh, full of junkies! Still the old needles, Rodge!'

I'd rather work than be stuck down here. All I've done since

13

my accident is edge the Mona Lisa in the toilet with bordering and paint the lounge and look after the taps and the water-pipes and mark the sheets and pillowslips for my wife in Indian ink so they won't get lost in the laundry. I've a gallon of white paint left. I'm going to paint the cupboards in the kitchen. It's like doing time.

What I want before I die is a nice little cottage in the South of Ireland with four acres for a field and a tropical garden. I've never seen Ireland except from the deck of a ship but I've been told the houses are whitewashed and I want to buy a white-washed house with thick walls and two-foot open fireplaces and a slate roof. I'll build a conservatory with a Perspex roof and shelves all round for potted plants and I'll cement the floor so we can sit on deckchairs. You'll have to come through the conservatory to get to the front door. And I'm going to buy a male donkey and some chickens and a goat and I'm going to brush the donkey every day and keep it indoors at night. I'll put hay down and I'll put boards on the flagstones next to the kitchen where it will be warm and I'm going to have a doorway where it can go in the field. For the dogs I'm going to put down chain netting. Two twenty-five-foot rolls will make a big pen. I don't want them disturbing farmers' cattle and sheep. And I'll have wire for the cat because she catches rabbits. When we was in Kent she sat for hours and hours outside rabbit holes.

I'll take some of our furniture with me and my tools. I'll take the big mahogany sideboard with the buffet and I'll take the fumed oak sideboard, the beds, the carved Indian elephants I got cheap in Leicester Square, and the brass candlesticks. I'll take some paraffin lamps, some tables, the roll of lino and my wife's big white marble statue of Saint Teresa. I want them put in a container so they can go on the ship and be delivered to the door. My copper Buddha I'm taking personally, wrapped up in a bag I'll have on my back because I can't carry suit-cases. And when I get there I'm going to write and write till I die because I want to achieve something in the form of books what other people can read.

14

India and Africa

I was born 'on the strength'—that means 'in the British Army'—in the year 1905, the 12th of July, in a little village called Chaubuttia in the foothills of the Himalayas.

My father was a farrier sergeant and veterinary surgeon in the First Royal Dragoons, a cavalry regiment, a crack regiment. Time after time I stood in my bare feet to watch him tent-pegging and playing polo. He looked splendid in his uniform and spurs playing polo on a well-groomed charger. For tent-pegging there was a peg in the ground and he charged along on a horse with a lance about twelve foot long with two ribbons on the end, and he never missed a peg. He could chloroform a horse, operate on a horse, pull tape-worms out of a horse. He could tell the age of a horse by its teeth. He used to teach me all about hands—a horse was so many hands high and so many hands small. He made horseshoes on an anvil with a hammer and fitted them on the horses' feet and cooled them off in oil and water. He had a leather apron on. You could smell the hooves of horses burning where he put on the red-hot iron. He never worked on the anvil till he'd had his pint of beer. Ten pints of beer would be nothing to my father. He could drink beer like I drink tea and I drink twenty-five cups a day. Once for a bet he lay on the floor with his head on a straw cushion and drank a barrel of beer, about five gallons, through a rubber pipe connected to the bung.

When I was born my mother was taken away from me to hospital, an Indian and a soldier with her, in what they call a tonga garry pulled along by oxen through the hills on a dirt path road. She had malaria so bad that her hair came out when

15

the nurses combed it. There was a Kaffir woman in the compound, a big Kaffir woman with two big breasts. She had a chotababbee strapped to her back in a cloth and she fed the chotababbee on one breast thrown over her shoulder and she fed me on the other and I was brought up by this Kaffir woman until my mother came home.

The regiment travelled about. We didn't stay in one place too long. When it became very hot we moved from the towns and went up in the hills. When it got cooler we come back in the towns again. I was registered on a birth certificate in Lucknow. My father said, 'We'll call him Sidney Arthur Brahma.' He gave me an Indian name after Brahma the bull. The Brahma bull has a hump and I had a large head.

We lived in married quarters so my mother had a dhobi woman to do the washing and a punkah wallah who lay on the floor and put a rope round his toe and pulled a fan. Then there was the bobbagee who cooked. We shared our bobbagee with two or three other families. He'd come across to our bungalow with a big tray on his head and waving a big knife over the meat to keep away the kite hawks. We called them 'shite hawks'. They were like vultures, two foot across. If you went out of the house eating a slice of bread they'd swoop down and take the bread right out of your fingers and probably tear your fingers to pieces too.

The bobbagees used to sit cross-legged in a circle smoking their hubble-bubbles. In the East they don't drink alcohol but they smoke opium from the poppy and cannabis which comes from marijuana, the tip of the plant. I knew cannabis when I was a child of six. The hubble-bubble is a little clay pipe about eight inches long and the bobbagees cup their hands round the bowl and when they've finished and they go back to the cookhouse to work they dig a hole in the muti, the dirt, and they bury these hubble-bubbles in the ground till they come out again so they'll be nice and cool. Once I went to the circle and broke it up where they was all smoking their hubble-bubbles and yapping away. I hit our cook on the head with a street-sweeper's broom.

The sweeper in India is the lowest class of Indian, a very very low caste, and the cook went to my mother in tears and he said, 'Memsahib! Memsahib! Brahma hit me on the head with sweeper's broom! He break my caste! He break my caste!' It's the same today. There's a caste system in India that nobody can break. It's worse than Northern Ireland and the Catholics and Protestants.

In the army everything was whitewashed. The bathrooms were whitewashed. Even the glasshouse was whitewashed. The toilets, which were far away from the bungalows, they were all whitewashed. You sat on a plank with a hole in it and everything went into the ground six foot deep. When the trench got full we covered it with muti and in three or four hours the troops would dig another trench and carry the hut over that. I remember going to the toilet in the dark about a hundred and fifty yards from the bungalow, all wild on the edge of the khudds. Nobody wanted to go there because of stray tigers. I heard a scratching on the door and when I opened it there were about forty rhesus monkeys and baboons showing their teeth at me. I run home with my trousers and my braces hanging down and the monkeys chasing me.

I'd a worse experience. One night I was lying in bed while my mother and father went to an officers' ball. There was curry on the table and rooti, that's bread, and monkeys jumped through the window. They were all over the place eating this food. I was so frightened I put my head under the bedclothes. My father come back for a box of matches and chased every monkey out of the house. They scattered left and right.

The only school I remember going to in India was the Murray Military School. We'd a white schoolteacher to teach us English. We stopped at twelve o'clock and sang a song called 'Marching Home to Dinner':

> Home to dinner, home to dinner;
> Hear the bells, hear the bells.
> Smoking hot potatoes, smoking hot potatoes;
> Ding dong bells, ding dong bells.

17

Up in the Murray Hills was a seat. I often used to think as a small boy, 'What a peculiar seat!' You'd to put your foot over the top and jump inside and sit towards the tree. Somebody in the army built it for lovers and sweethearts. It was called the Green Seat. You wouldn't go up there at night time—there was leopards and tigers. But in the day time when the sun was shining there was only gibbons and baboons and rhesus monkeys.

I went fishing with my father several times on the banks of the river Jumna. He took an Express rifle. He'd say, 'See that crocodile over there? I'm going to hit it right between the eyes!' When he shot a crocodile he got it out of the water with a rope and then he'd settle down to fish.

One crocodile caused a serious accident to my mother. My father got some native boys to carry it home and they gutted it and he cleaned it with alum and then the natives stuffed it with cotton wool, sewed it up and put it in an old wash-house, stood it up in a corner. My mother went in the wash-house to get the bath and when she saw the crocodile she had a shock and jumped back and gashed her arm on the lock which meant eleven stitches.

One day my father was fishing and I was rolling the bread, rooti, and putting it on his three hooks for him when all of a sudden he said, 'Brahma, get the basket and get the tackle quick and get away from here! There's a rattlesnake behind us somewhere in the bushes! Can you hear the rattle?!' And I heard the rattle.

I've been on a tiger hunt twice. My father used to say, 'No, no, no!' but twice he gave in. Once I went on an elephant with a Maharaja and officers of the regiment through the elephant grass, six feet high, the long grass of Bengal. I can feel myself rocking in the howdah. Round the tiger are beaters beating frying pans and old tin cans. They've been paid one silver rupee each. We don't see the tiger. The elephants are the first to spot it and they start flapping their ears and swinging their trunks and trumpeting. The beaters run up the nearest tree or get back to the village. Then someone takes a crack shot at the tiger with a rifle but nobody gets near till they're

sure the tiger's dead. An elephant is made to put a leg on the
tiger to break its ribs. The Indians skin the tiger, scrape the
skin, wash it with alum, stretch it out in the sun.

My father used to go out in a jingler, a little pony and trap.
A native was driving and my father used to sit in the jingler
with his gun and shoot peacocks. He cut the tail feathers off
with an open razor and put the peacocks in a bag and my
mother roasted them and stuffed them. He also caught butterflies with a fly-dodging net to win competitions. He caught
beautiful butterflies and pinned them down in glass cases. The
pins had a little tiny coloured head on the end of them like
marble.

Today I've my labrador and boxer and Siamese cat but in
India you couldn't keep many pets. You could only keep a
parrot or a non-poisonous snake in a glass box because other
pets would get killed by wilder animals or else they'd catch
dysentery. Not just pets caught dysentery. All the family in India
had it. My brother George, my brother Tom, my brother Fred,
my sister Winnie had it. I had it. My mother had it. My father
had it. It comes away from you like hot water. You're red raw.

We went to Simla and Cashmere. We used to go in the
bazaars. The bazaars were beautiful. It's beautiful to see the
brass chatties and the lanterns made by the Chinese, big paper
lanterns, and the fireworks. I have never seen fireworks since
like them! When I first come to England we had Paynes's and
Brocks's. They made fireworks, but nothing compared to these
Chinese crackers. Me, Tom and George and Winnie used to buy
three pounds' worth in weight at a time. We threw them in the
garden and we threw them outside the controlment. When we
were in Cashmere there used to be two big Sikhs stood with
their lances and a white rope all round and all the ladies—it
was a marriage market—and all the gentlemen were having a
moonlight dance and they all had these paper lanterns burning from China. Seats were all round and you could go in and
watch the dancing which happened about every three months.
The two Sikhs used to give us a bag of sweets and once we

19

took with us a big packet of fireworks. Now these fireworks were all tied by the wicks. They were just plain red fireworks two inches long and we unwrapped them, unplaited the wicks with a kind of a darning needle and threw them up in the air and they each made a louder noise than a thunderbolt. I've never heard fireworks that made such a noise. Very dangerous and only two inches long, just like a bullet. We threw them amongst the dancers and men chased us out past the two Sikhs.

The Maharajas lived in palaces. It was like a dream—beautiful women, beautiful swimming pools, diamonds, gold, emeralds. The Maharaja of Hyderabad had tame tigers and a hundred fighting elephants. Fifty elephants in a line going through the city was a sight never to be forgotten. All the people lined the roadside and the Maharaja and his favourite wife rode past and the Maharaja waved to everybody, to all his subjects. The elephants were painted gold. Some had their tusks inlaid with gold.

In all parts of India there are big stockades made of bamboo and trees and inside you'd never see less than two hundred and fifty elephants. As a boy I used to climb up these stockades. They're about ten feet high. The elephants were quite tame. They were working elephants. They used to pull timber, they used to pull ricks, they used to build roads and there used to be big long ropes or chains fixed to the elephant and the elephant would pull a ton rock along or teak trees and it did all the work with its tusks or with its trunk or with its pulling power. They used to feed the elephants with sugar cane an inch and a half to two inches thick, chopped with a churi. They used to cut it in one foot lengths and throw it over the stockades to the elephants. I climbed up the stockades and fed them too. They'd curl their trunks up and take the sugar cane gently out of my hand, put it in their mouth with their trunk and chew it, outer skin and everything.

Up at the top of the khudds in a place called Assam was tea gardens, all terraces with women, and Indians with

20

guns to protect them, picking tea all in their saris and in their lovely gold bangles, a little diamond in their noses and some with the caste of marriage, a little red spot in the centre of the forehead like lipstick. The most beautiful women in the world today aren't Western, they're Moslems. They've long natural black hair. They don't smoke cigarettes. They don't smoke the hubble-bubble. They don't take drugs. They've got a nice sleek walk, they walk just like a gazelle. They can make beautiful carpets with their long narrow fingers and can do any kind of knitting and crochet work. They've skins like velvet. They make English girls look coarse and rough. I've been to bed with dozens. When you're lying on top of them they recite the Koran. It's beautiful. I met one two years ago outside the Chicken Inn.

One day I borrowed the cook's old bicycle. It had no mud-guards on it and it was too big for me and I used to pedal on it standing up. I pushed it up the khudds till I reached level ground and I heard a scream and I saw a commotion in the tea gardens. I thought, 'The best thing I can do is get down the hill as quick as I can and get in the house and tell my mother and father.' The same evening we found out that a tiger had come into the tea gardens and flew at a woman and knocked her down and killed her with its claws, and it flew at another woman, tore all her sari off her and killed her, and a third woman it dragged for about two miles to its lair by a watercourse. The next day, just like Jesse James, there was a notice put on all the trees: 5,000 RUPEES REWARD FOR THE CAPTURE OF MAN-EATING TIGER, and many of the soldiers went out with rifles looking for this man-eater but they couldn't find it.

One day too there was a child put on the verandah of a house because it was crying. The mother just put it outside for a few minutes to stop it from crying and that child was never seen again. All we know is that the child was carried away by some wild beast, probably by some old toothless tiger that smelt it down-wind. A man-eater will attack anything. It will attack

21

an elephant. It will attack a buffalo. They're crazy when they're man-eaters. They've tasted human blood and it turns them.

People ask me in this country have I ever seen the Indian rope trick. No, there's no such thing as the Indian rope trick. But there's the mango tree trick: a little boy comes along with an old man and they ask for paises and rupees and they put a mango seed in some soil in a plant pot, cover the plant pot with a cloth, pull up the cloth six foot high—and there's a mango tree with fruit growing on it! How this is done I do not know.

But all over India there are snake charmers. They play a flute to a cobra in a basket. I've been bit by cobras. One bit me on the knee in the garden. We had big green pumpkins with big leaves and when the monsoons came it was lovely to see the rain coming down on them for ten minutes and the sun shining and in the sky two or three rainbows. I remember the sun was shining after a heavy rain and it was about eighty-five to ninety degrees in the shade and my mother said, 'Go outside and get a ripe pumpkin and bring it in,' and I went outside with a knife to get the pumpkin and as I bent down a cobra struck me. It was coiled up under a leaf sheltering from the rain. It just put its head out and put two great fangs into me like six inch nails and injected serum. I shouted, 'Mam!' and then in three minutes I was unconscious and the regimental doctor had to see me. Another time I climbed two cypress trees grown together like twins. At the top was a nest. My father was working on an anvil in the blacksmith's shop. The tree was just outside and I thought, 'I wonder what's in that nest. Is there any eggs or young birds?' and I put my hand in and woke up a cobra, a white cobra with a white black-spotted hood, and it inflated its hood and it struck me unconscious and I was taken to hospital and I had to have my right hand cauterised. On the front of my right hand there's a scar. And there's one on my back—a cobra again. I was after a long green snake for a pet and I didn't know there was a cobra behind me. I was down among the flowers and mohair ferns

22

by a watercourse and this cobra put its fangs right in my back.

One day my mother and father went to a big 'do' for the army and somebody got through our bungalow window and took my mother's cabin trunk, her ditty-box. In it was all her wedding clothes. The thieving bobbagees get through a window, their bodies stripped and covered with cheetah fat so you can't hold them they're so slippery. If a soldier of the regiment caught a thief he was stretched out hand and foot on a charpoy and left in the sun all day absolutely naked and at night time taken off and shot. Thieves tried in an Indian court had their fingers or a hand cut off so the soldiers thought it better to shoot them. The British always believed in suppressing the natives. That's how they kept India as long as they did.

There were people in India dying. In Calcutta you could walk on the Howrah Bridge that crosses the Ganges, the Holy River, and find dead people there every morning. That's where they went to die when they knew they were sick and there was no cure for them—old people, emaciated people, people dying of starvation. At Benares I helped take lakri, dry wood, off the boats to make funeral pyres. Bodies were lifted onto the pyres. Six o'clock in the morning you would see the blue smoke coming up from about twenty-two pyres. The haze of the blue smoke used to flow down the Ganges right by the walls of the old walled city of Benares.

When I was six we sailed from Bombay to Durban. Many years before we left, Queen Victoria gave my father a metal box full of chocolates. She walked right along the line of troops and gave him this tin box. It was red and gold with a bust of Queen Victoria on and my father used to keep his medals and all his knick-knacks in this tin box.

To get to Bombay we was a week in one train. We never left that train for a week. We travelled on the light railway and when the man used to pull the rope to make the whistle of the engine blow that meant 'Pull your blinds down!' because we went over big girder bridges hundreds of feet above gorges. When he blew the whistle three times that meant 'You can let

23

your blinds up now!' Sometimes people used to throw themselves through the windows and commit suicide in the river down below which was full of crocodiles and alligators.

You saw monkeys travelling on the passing goods trains, tearing open the bags for food, but the nicest sight I saw was women camping with all their belongings on the railway station platforms, sat down beside little fireplaces made of brick, cooking pots of curry and laying out their chappatis.

There were thieves knocking about in Bombay and they called these the Bombay Stranglers. They could strangle a man or a woman in three seconds with a piece of wire or a piece of silk. My sister Elsie, who now lives in Worsley, was born in Bombay.

We sailed to Durban on a P and O ship, the SS *Rohilla*. While I was running about with the other kids my mother sat on the stairway on the main deck holding the rails she was so seasick. The ship was rolling port and starboard and turning over and over. When we stopped at Mauritius a boat come alongside and threw a rope up to us and we pulled up a basket of the best and biggest pineapples in the world. We ate them till our lips were cracked.

We landed at Durban and went straight into barracks. One regiment moved out and we moved in. At Durban were the rickshaw wallahs, Zulus with big horns on their heads and big feathers. They were all lined up like taxis outside a station. That's the first thing you see—the Zulus, the finest built people and the friendliest people in the whole of Africa. When they're running along the road with you to take you to your destination they're saying in broken English, 'I hope you may die. I hope you may die. I hope you may die.' That's the only English they can speak: 'I hope you may die. I hope you may die. I hope you may die.' The only krait I ever saw in my life was in a zoo in Durban. They had a snake pit there with about twenty krait. A Zulu used to come every day and pick them up with a stick like a pair of long tongs. Then he used to grab them by the back of the head and squeeze the throat so the serum from the fangs went into a bottle. A cobra can fill a dessert-spoonful of serum and a krait, as deadly as a cobra, fills a teaspoon.

My sister Elizabeth was born in South Africa. We called her Betty. She was born at Roberts Heights. There was a diamond mine under a field at Roberts Heights. And there was a big blockhouse about four feet thick with four open windows each side where you could fire through. It was full of rocks and I climbed in and I found plenty of bullets and a couple of old rusty bayonets. We were in Durban, Roberts Heights, Johannesburg and Capetown. We moved about with the army. The army was keeping order after the Boer War like the troops now in Northern Ireland. When we came home to England we'd been in South Africa three years. It's a clean country is South Africa, and the flowers can beat any in the world. One other thing—the moon of a night time. The moon was lovely and bright. You could read a newspaper by the light of the moon.

Manchester

We sailed home from South Africa on the SS *Dufferin*. We landed at Southampton and when we landed at Southampton it was foggy and a damp drizzle was coming down and all the families with their luggage and packs got on the one train to Manchester and, do you know what they did with us? they didn't bring us into Victoria Station or London Row Station, they brought us into Liverpool Row Station where the cattle trains used to come, and it was early in the morning, about four o'clock in the morning, so the public couldn't see us. That's the way the army map worked. They brought us down a ramp made of cobblestones near Liverpool Row, off Deansgate. But there was one thing about it, they had a house ready for each of the families. We went to No. 9, Sanderson Street, a house with seven rooms upstairs and three down. The rent was seven and six a week and it was a lovely house but it was too big for my mother and too close to my father's relatives.

My mother could never go near the Rogers. They were rough and tough. They did boxing and my mother was more of a gentle person. My father's father had a big beard hanging down to his belly button nearly and he loved his pint of beer. One day he came to us and my mother said, 'What do you want here? Father's at work.' He said, 'He wants me to live here.' My mother said, 'You'd better wait till he comes back.' So he waited in the kitchen and lit his pipe and started spitting in the fire. My mother said, 'I don't know what I'm going to do with him,

Sid.' I said, 'Put him in the parlour.' When my father got home he went in the parlour and took him out to buy him a drink. When they come home my mother had a fire waiting in the parlour. In the parlour there was a lovely old-fashioned antique clock on a beautiful marble mantelpiece and two magnificent vases painted with red roses, and in the window were aspidistras, pedigree—some were variegated, some were all green. Instead of my grandfather going through the kitchen and down the stoop to the backyard to have a pee, he peed on my mother's fire. Next day she said, 'You'd better pack up and get out.' He'd done it all over the coal and she had to keep the windows open for days to let the smell out.

But one thing I thought very nice about Manchester was people knocking on windows at five o'clock in the morning, old people with twelve-foot bamboo poles with the ribs of umbrellas tied to them tapping on the windows. They were called knockers-up. My father later employed one. It was a woman. She wouldn't leave the window alone until you got out of bed and said, 'All right. Thank you very much.' She used to rattle these umbrella ribs on the end of her pole, and she had a black shawl fastened over her head with a safety-pin because the mornings were very cold.

My first job was lather boy in Ward's in Collyhurst Street, a barber's shop. I lathered the men and Mr Ward used to shave them. Then Mr Ward said, 'You can shave them, Sid,' so I had to shave them. I used to shout, 'Next, please! Shave, sir?' There was one customer, he wouldn't answer, just get in the chair and fall asleep. I was nervous about shaving him because he had an enormous Adam's apple and when he snored his Adam's apple would work up and down. Once I nicked it and blood started flowing and I had to get cotton wool and plaster, but the man come in the next day and he said, 'Shave me again but don't touch here.' He had confidence in me.

Next I worked in a hat shop called Nicholson's on Rochdale Road. My duties were to deg the floor with a degging can and then sweep it up and clean it. When Mr Nicholson came it was my duty to make him a cup of tea, have a cup of tea myself, and then I'd stand outside the shop with a cadey on me or a bowler or a trilby and talk to people as they passed. 'Lovely hats here! Very cheap! All styles and fashions!', 'This bowler is silk lined!'

One morning I went to work. I opened the shop and I waited till about ten o'clock and Mr Nicholson hadn't come. I went into the backyard and into the lavatory to have a pee. The door was ajar. When I pushed the door open it swung back in my face. I pushed it again. It swung back in my face. Then I saw a pair of shoes about a foot from the floor. I pulled the bolt back on the backyard door and run down the back entry and running down this entry I found a policeman. I said, 'Will you come and help me, please? There's a pair of shoes hanging in Nicholson's lavatory!' The policeman took his time. 'Don't hurry,' he says. 'You go for another policeman, will you? Go to Willert Street and find another policeman to help me.' He went to the lavatory and he found Mr Nicholson hanging. Then another four or five policemen come and they cut him down from a wooden beam. I don't know what his trouble was to take his life as he did. He was one of my best bosses. He never bullied me.

While I was at Nicholson's we moved from Sanderson Street to Lodge Street and from Lodge Street to No. 9, Pexton Street, a nice corner house on the gable end where Norman my youngest brother was born, the only child in the family to be born in England. The house is still there now and the street is called Erasmus Street, up Fitzgeorge Street, Collyhurst, Manchester. There was a factory right by us and that factory was Wright and Holmes Brothers, mechanical organ builders. They built from scratch these beautiful big Wakes organs what went on the fairground with all the statuettes, men and women turning round, their arms moving, their legs moving, banging kettle-drums and a conductor waving a stick.

When the *Lusitania* was torpedoed in 1915 and Nurse Cavell was shot, the people started breaking all our windows. They thought we were foreigners because we were new and never used to mix with anybody and wore white tropical clothes the same as we did in India and Africa. The police from Willert Street Police Station stopped them and said, 'Mr Rogers is fighting out in France and he's already lost three brothers.'

My father had to come out of the war after one year and seven months because he got a whiff of mustard gas at a place called Passchendaele when the wind was blowing towards the Allies. He had to go into Ashton Infirmary. When he recuperated he joined the Corps of Commissionaires, Spring Gardens. He worked at Deacon's Bank, the Ford Motor Co., and the Free Trade Hall and at Tattersalls ring, Haydock Park, on the racecourse. He used to bring home two tickets a week for the Free Trade Hall. I used to go and see the Brand Lane Concerts with the Hallé Orchestra under Sir Hamilton Harty and Sir John Henry Wood. I used to sit upstairs in the fifteen shilling seats, free of charge, among men with black astrakhan collars who knew more about music than me. It was classical, beautiful. Then there was the concerts at Queen's Park, Prestwich and Bury where you could see the Irlam O'er the Heights Band and the Black Dyke Band, prize bands. But the best band of the lot was the Foden Band. The Foden steamroller factory had a band and it was a pedigree band. Manchester had the best brass bands in the world.

Before they could get in to the body works at Ford's every man had to show my father their badge, the Ford Flivver badge. The Ford Flivver cost £51 right off the assembly line. It was the first Ford car made in England and my Dad was at the factory. I was about fourteen when I met John Ford. My father said, 'Are you coming down today, Brahma?' I said, 'Why?' He said, 'Henry Ford's coming from America.' I saw Henry Ford. He was tall, grey-haired, and he was dressed all in white—white trousers, white coat.

The only pity of the Flivver was, as more and more cars came on the road, they took the tramcars off Rochdale Road and put trolley-buses instead. As a boy after the First World

War I used to run up the stairs of the tramcars and sit in the front and get the wind and the breeze. There was a man we called Daft Sam. He'd bend down in the middle of the tram-lines and move his hands in circles when he knew a tram was coming. The tram driver used to sound his gong—ding-ding! ding-ding!—to get him out of the way, but Daft Sam would stop the tram. The driver had to put the auto-sander on and the sand would come in and make the brake tight. He said, 'You bleeding fool! Get out of the way! Get out of the way!' and Sam would stand aside and wave and say, 'Bye-bye! Bye-bye!'

There was horse-and-carts in them days. On May Day they used to dress the horses up and put ribbons and florettes made of silk on them and comb and plait their tails, and they used to parade them up Rochdale Road, Oldham Street, Oxford Road and Stretford Road. There were some beautiful big horses. You'd be surprised how big the horseshoes were compared to the ones on the chargers of my father's cavalry days. These were the shires. Some of them could pull two to three ton. That was the idea in Lancashire of cobblestones, so the horses could grip.

There was also the donkeys of the rag and bone men who gave balloons to the children, balloons on a stick or string, in exchange for rags, bones, old clothes, shoes, hats. Or they gave the women brown and white stones to kneel down and colour their steps, what we called 'donkey-stone the step'. They used to shout, 'Stones for blue mould bones!' We called them 'donkey men'.

My mother's name before she married was Winifred Love. Her father lived in Droitwich, Worcestershire. He done forty years on the railways and when he retired the Railway gave him a cottage and about two acres of orchard, beautiful plums and apples, and he kept pigs and hens and cocks. My mother said, 'Would you like to go to Grandad Love's for a weekend?' I said, 'Yes,' and my father said, 'While you're there, ask him to give you the two baskets of chickens he promised me.'

So I went to this cottage in Droitwich and who should I see

but a big eighteen stone man with a big paunch sat outside on a big form, and the cottage chimney was smoking. I said, 'Excuse me. Is your name David Love?' He said, 'Yes. You're Sidney, aren't you?' I said, 'That's right. I've come from Manchester—No. 9, Pexton Street. My mother sent me.' He introduced me to his wife. This was his third wife. He'd buried two and this one was six foot tall, handsome looking with a big aquiline nose, but she had no breasts and she seldom spoke because she was all the time busy in the house, busy in the garden, busy in the orchard. The only time she spoke was when she lit the oil lamp of a night time on the table in the kitchen. I said to David Love, 'My father says you promised him two baskets of chickens,' and he said, 'Yes, that's right, and I'll give you five cocks as well, big cocks.' One of these cocks used to jump on our wall every morning and cockadoodledoo. It was a fighting cock, a beautiful big cock with big claws and a red comb and at five o'clock every morning he used to stand on the yard wall right on the corner and everybody knew.

My father loved birds. Every morning, except when it was cold and wet, he used to hang about twelve cages outside on the wall. He had a collection of Yorkshire Roller canaries, lovely slim-lined canaries, but we had one bird that beat the lot and that was a skylark called Jim. All day long, especially when the sun was shining on his cage, he used to be whistling. I used to bath the canaries. I blew down a little tube with some water. It was a fine spray and the canaries would ruffle themselves.

During the war I used to wait at the edge of the pavement in Collyhurst, the hub of Manchester. At seven o'clock every evening a string of war ambulances used to come up Rochdale Road and we'd stand there, all clapping and cheering. Some of the ambulances had British wounded in them. Some had German prisoners of war. Most of the prisoners went to Alfred Street School, Harpurhey, three quarters of a mile from where we stood. We could see them next day in the playground and we used to talk to them through the bars and they used to give us souvenirs for cigarettes. They'd give us badges, old caps with two buttons on the front, and helmets with the eagle on. I'd the finest collection of German souvenirs. I had swords. I had daggers.

One night my father took all my souvenirs, went out and threw them over the wall right behind Berry's Blacking Works into the Cut. That was where the Irk, the Irwell, went underground before coming up again at Smedley Lane. I know the river from beginning to end. A vapour used to come off it. It smelt. One day the water would be red. Next day it would be brown. Next day it would be ink black. The reason was the bleach and chemical works put all their overspill in pipes into the water. Some parts were deep. Some parts were shallow. I used to cross over for money. I'd take wagers off all the gangs, fasten the money in my trousers' pocket and wade across, passing the old rusty bicycles and the spring mattresses.

Sometimes I used to take an old bedsheet and climb over the wall of Queen's Park Cemetery at the bottom of Conran Street and start dancing in the middle of the pathway with the white sheet on me and night after night people would say, 'Look at the ghost! Look at the ghost!' I used to flitter from grave to grave, then disappear over the wall again, wrap up the sheet and stick it up my blue jumper and run away. The police caught me in the end. They were in the cemetery and they said 'You're the ghost, aren't you? We've got you now!' and they took me to Willert Street Police Station and my mother had to bail me out.

When my father came home drunk he'd row with my mother. I've seen him throw a full plate of dinner she'd kept hot for him into the fireplace. This used to anger me and I used to swear at him and shout at him. Then he'd get up and throw something at me and I'd run out the front door like a March hare and I'd come back the back way and Mother would say, 'Don't come in yet, Sid. He's in here. He's in a bad temper still. Wait till he goes to bed.'

He used to get very drunk at the weekends, especially when he was commissionaire on the turnstiles at Haydock Park racecourse. My mother used to say, 'Sid, will you go down to Harry Minns's?' and I used to go into the bar amongst all the women and all the men and I used to shout, 'George, come home to your wife!' and he'd say, 'Get out, you little bugger, else I'll give you a damn good hiding!' He never liked me calling him by his first name. I said, 'George, your wife's waiting at home for you. My mother is waiting with the dinner in the oven while you're buying pints for these people.' Half an hour afterwards he'd be staggering up the hill and my mother would say, 'Go and help him, Sid,' and I used to run out and get hold of his arm. Later she'd say, 'Go upstairs quietly and go down his pockets. He's asleep in bed.' His trousers was on one of the brass knobs of the bed and I used to go down his pockets and take a lot of silver and come down and say, 'Here you are, Mother.' I'd keep sixpence or a shilling for myself. The old man never twigged it for years.

Every Monday morning my mother used to collect all our best clothes and I used to take them to Charlie Reid's pawn shop at the corner of Churnet Street opposite Dobson's, the chemists. I took the bundles to the pledge department. Bundles were only allowed to be in for three months. After three months if you wanted your clothes back you had to get a certificate signed by a magistrate. But my mother got our clothes out every Friday because on Sunday she sent all her children to church. We had to go to church on Sunday in the morning and on Sunday in the evening and I was the only one that crept out the back door half time. My sister Elsie used to say to my mother, 'Sid came out half time. He wouldn't watch the full service and he wouldn't sing no hymns,' and my mother used to tell me how I was a heathen. My mother in them days was a spiritualist. She met this Welshman near the Three Tuns in Topley Street and this Welshman was a medium who did article reading or table-rappings and she came home laughing and dancing or fascinated. 'I've heard the truth!' she said and she turned into a medium and took seven and sixpence a time from gullible people in the parlour and gave out prayer books and got in touch with the dead. My father didn't believe in spiritualism. He said, 'The only spirits I believe in are in a bottle.' And *I* didn't believe in spiritualism so when she told me how I was a heathen I said, 'What are you?! You're a spiritualist!'

In 1937, before my father died, I went with my mother to see him at Ashton Infirmary. We went on a bus and when I went in the ward and sat at the side of the bed I could not believe a seventeen stone ten man could get down to about eight stone. He was blind and being eaten away with cancer. He had tubes up his nose, tubes in his mouth, and he had an ordinary cotton shirt belonging to the hospital, no collar, a union shirt worn by poor paid workers. I was so disgusted to see my father in such a state, I walked out of the hospital. I said to my mother, 'Mam, I'll wait for you outside. I can stand no more. You wonder why I don't go to church now, Mam, do you?!' Mother said, 'Don't be uncouth, boy! Don't be uncouth!' I said, 'Mam, I don't go to church because of things like letting Dad die like this with cancer. It shouldn't be!' He got ten shillings a week off the British Legion, and his Long Service Pension, thirty-two years, died with him. When he died my mother said, and I'll never forget it because my father being an old soldier never went to church in his life, he sang hymn after hymn . . .

Charlie Reid, the pawnbroker, was a retired CID man. His home was in Blackley. There was only him and his mother. Our Tom worked for him for ten years in the pledge department. He used to sit on the counter reading little tiny novels called *Sexton Blake*. My brother must have read every Sexton Blake that was published. One day he came off ill and I took his place and I was there a month. Every Monday morning the women would come in with bundles of clothes and pledge them for three and six, seven and six, ten shillings. Sometimes jewellery come in. Charlie used to test the gold with a little piece of acid out of a bottle. If it went green it wasn't gold.

I liked working in a pawnshop so much that I went to May's pawnshop, a bigger pawnshop, lower down Rochdale Road.

I worked upstairs throwing bundles down and catching the bundles thrown up to me to stack the racks and put a ticket on. After that I worked at Piggy Riley's. The reason why he got the name Piggy Riley was one day a woman came in and pawned a pig's head in a bundle. The old man wouldn't employ anybody and he was too lazy to open the bundle. After a few months it began to stink and when he went upstairs he found the pig's head in the bundle.

One day a man come round to our house with a peaked cap and a black raincoat and he said, 'I'm the School Board. How many children have you got, Mrs Rogers? We've found out your children don't go to school. How old is this boy?' My mother said, 'He was born out in India in 1905 and now he's going out to work, he's doing odd jobs.' 'Well,' said the School Board, 'he should go to school and get a bit of English.' My mother said, 'We speak English very well, probably better than you do, and if you stand arguing with me round the door I'll bring my husband. He's only in bed.' So she went into the parlour where my father was sleeping in his woollen combs. My father didn't give a damn about anybody and he got to the steps of the front door and the School Board was running down the hill.

This School Board persecuted me for weeks. In the end I went to St Oswald's—gas jets on the wall, old stone steps with iron spikes so kids couldn't slurr down. The top floor was one big open schoolroom with five classes in it. In the middle of the floor was reposing a beautiful light oak desk and behind that sat a grey-haired gentleman in striped trousers and black vicuna coat and a gold watch and chain. His name was Mr Horrocks.

I went to school for only two weeks in England. I'll tell you why. This woman of about forty-five called Miss Gradwell used to put a map of Ireland on the board and tell us the names of the Irish counties to teach us geography. That didn't interest me. I'd travelled all over India and all over South Africa as a baby and I intended to travel the rest of the world later and see it for myself. So Miss Gradwell said to me, 'When we have geography lessons I'll give you a book and you can sit on your own on the corner.' But there was a girl named Ivy Ward and she was a blonde and she'd two plaits. She was a snob. She didn't like me because I was rough and always had grass snakes from Rosewood in my pockets. One day I left my book down and I said I'd like to come in the class and Miss Gradwell said, 'That's very nice of you, Sidney. Very nice of you,' and while she was pointing out the different places like Cork and Dublin on the map of Ireland I cut off one of Ivy Ward's plaits. Her father come down to our house and started bullying my mother. He kept a picture-framing shop in Conran Street. My mother said, 'You'd better come tomorrow and see my husband,' and he come to see my father and my father said, 'I've no responsibility for this boy if he doesn't want to go to school,' so I didn't have to go to school no more.

Now my favourite man them days used to be on the silent films. I went to Dickie Banks's picture house which we used to call Flecky Winnies' and a woman used to sit on a lemonade box and play the piano and the floor was scattered with sand. As I see it today there was gas jets burning on the wall, no mantels on them, and all the kids were stamping their feet because a film had broken down and she was playing all these old English songs. Then Samson come on the screen and we had to read the words—it was a silent picture. And that was Dickie Banks's, what we called Flecky Winnies' because the place was lousy. It had a corrugated roof and corrugated iron sides this picture house but they showed the most marvellous films you could ever see in your life, silent films— Pearl White, Bill Hart, the cowboy, and we saw Charlie Chaplin and we saw all the old stars. And that day it didn't used to cost much for you to go to the pictures. It used to cost about threepence to fourpence to sixpence, the best seats, and I used to get in a seat with all the girls and all the kids. They were a lot younger than me and I used to go right in the front so I could see the picture clear. The old woman would come in.

She'd sit on the box and play the piano and there would come Sansonio, the strongest man in Italy, handsome, beautiful, a black mass of black wavy hair, and he'd show you his chest and the muscles on his arms and I saw him knock a factory chimney over. I wept and wept and wept and I said, 'I'm going to be a muscleman myself.' He put his shoulder against an old factory chimney that had to be knocked down and they knocked one brick out of the chimney and he pushed so hard with his shoulder, his left shoulder, the whole factory chimney fell down and he jumped out of the way and the ground shook beneath him. And then he got on an iron bridge and while he was on the iron bridge he threw a net over the bridge onto the floor, a car drove into the net with four people in and he pulled it up with his muscles and his muscles stood out—dynamic tension, mind over matter. I learned this dynamic tension. You've got to control all your body, and I've got a good body today and I'm an old man. I can lift a hundredweight above my head, not with a grab, with a lift. I can break bricks on my wrist. I put a full brick on my wrist and break it with another brick and I can do fifty of those in less than five minutes. It's a knack.

Now Sansonio was the best but we had another Italian besides and his name was Maciste. Maciste was found in Genoa walking down the gangplank with two bales of cotton on, one bale on each shoulder. This man weighed about twenty-two stone and he could pick two men up with his hands. Buffalo was another weightlifter. And my God he could lift! He could lift anything!

I used to bite my nails right down to the wick and when I got home my fingers were bleeding. My mother said, 'Look at your hands! You're going crazy about weightlifting!' and I said to my mother, 'Mother, I've never seen men like this in my life before! What they can lift!' So my mother said, 'Well the best thing I'll do, I'll pay one and ninepence a week for a correspondence course and you can do mind over matter and weightlifting.'

Once, before I crossed the road in Collier Street and went in Flecky Winnies', I went to Barnes's, the herbalist's. I'd been constipated for weeks so my mother said, 'Go and get some sarsaparilla' there. On the counter at Barnes's they had a big lighthouse. Mrs Barnes used to turn a tap and out would come sarsaparilla, a penny a glass. I said, 'Could you give me a good black draught of opening medicine, Mrs Barnes?' and she gave me one in a big mug. She said, 'Now swallow that right back. That'll work you.' So I swallowed it right back and I'm ashamed to say when the film started I did everything in my trousers, my trousers was stuck to me. The woman next to me said, 'You're a dirty boy!' but my mother said, 'Never mind. I'll take your trousers into the back yard and wash them.'

At this period on the films apart from Sansonio and Maciste and Buffalo, there was also Bernarr McFadden, Alexander Zass—a Cossack—and Earl E. Leaderman. And we saw Houdini, the escapologist, doing his tricks in a box. He was thrown into a harbour in handcuffs and chains and he got out of the box, though the police and everyone saw the box was screwed down, and he come to the top of the water in less than two minutes.

So I did a weightlifting correspondence course with Charles Atlas and as well as that I joined a club at the corner of Livesey Street. It was one big vast gymnasium. For threepence you could get a cup of tea and a currant bun. You had parallel bars, vaulting horses, swings, everything for developing your body. I also joined Harpurhey Swimming Club. I won silver medals, I won barometers, I won hairbrushes, vases, all sorts for swimming in galas.

I was always a very strong and powerful swimmer. During the day time, if I wasn't working, I used to queue up at Osborne Street with other boys. They used to take their clogs off and their socks off and queue up to go into the baths free. They went with a school. The masters were there with them. I used to take my clogs off, take my socks off, put my hand on the pavement and black my face, dirty my feet and join the queue.

38

Mr Smith, the attendant who had red hair, said, 'Are you here again?' I said, 'Yes, I've come with a school.' He said, 'I know you don't go to school. You're not working today?' I said, 'No, not today and I'll be coming in again with the next crowd that queues up.' I learned to dive by reading books. I found it come natural to me. I took to the water like a duck. Later on I worked at Sale Lido teaching young ladies, middle-aged women, young men, young children how to swim at five and six a time. I held the young women under the chin, sometimes under the breast. I had a black costume on and Instructor on my chest.

Near our house in Pexton Street was one of the finest cabinet makers in England. His name was Kaminski. He was a Russian Jew, a weightlifter with a big black beard. He made a couch of ebony and ivory and he got £400 for the one couch, without cushions. He taught me how to do wood-carving with gouges and a mallet, how to use clamps on the table, how to mix the cake glue (4/6d a pound). When he taught me how to veneer I got a job at Freeland's, cabinet making. I veneered in Russian oak, fumed oak, walnut, canary wood (the best to work in), bastard mahogany, Honduras mahogany and coppelia mahogany —I worked in all these veneers for Freeland's with a veneering machine, sheering the veneer off the tree with a blade in a big tank of water. It would take me a week to match a set of doors for an exhibition wardrobe. I took the veneers, put them upside down and put knots in them with a knife. I invented a better glue than what we were using: I put a secret substance in and it's still used today. A Jewish gentleman took the patent off me for three pound.

I lost the top of a finger on the forecutting machine at Freeland's. I was doing bed-ends, the old spring beds with wooden sides, with a forecutter with two motors. I switched the machine off to get the shavings out from underneath. I got a buffalo— made of cow hide; you could pull it on its skis underneath to shovel the shavings up—and crawled under the machine forgetting the cutters. The cutters took about five minutes to stop

39

after being switched off (this one was three feet long and six inches wide and had four blades on it as sharp as razors) and I put my hand up. They gave me twenty-five pound compensation for losing the end of my finger.

After cabinet making I made clock cases, Westminster Whittington Chimes. Then I worked at a rubber works. There were about fifteen girls there. I was the only man. We did single texture and double texture for raincoats. I used to mix naphtha outside in a cistern, a galvanized water tank, for sticking the edges of the coats. It made my eyes run. It smelt of ammonia. I also did buttonholing and eyeletting for air vents.

My mother bought me a Lucas bicycle from Walsh's Post Office and General Stores at the corner of Libby Street facing Piggy Riley's. It had new North Road handlebars on it and a new carrier and a new Brummell's pump and a three-speed. It cost three pound ten and was worth at least ten pound the way I done it up. I used to ride from Manchester to Blackpool, fifty-five miles; Manchester to Liverpool, thirty-five miles; Manchester to Hebden Bridge, forty-six miles, taking my time, just pedalling along.

After I'd had the bike for about two years I took it down to Cheetham Hill Road to sell it because I wanted motorbikes. I left the cycle outside the door and went into this cycle shop and a Jewish gentleman come to me and said, 'What do you want?' I said, 'I want to sell a bicycle.' He said, 'Will you bring it inside the shop?' I said, 'Certainly.' I took it inside the shop and put it against the counter and he pretended to look at it. He says, 'You know, I've a lot of second-hand bicycles. I can't get shut of them. But if you hold on a minute I'll talk to my partner.' He went round the back and kept me waiting ten minutes and, who should walk into the shop, but two plain clothes policemen. He'd been on the telephone to the police! The first thing the CID said to me was, 'Where have you got this bicycle from?' I said, 'My mother got it for me from Walsh's Post Office.' 'Come with us to your mother,' they said, 'and bring the cycle with you.' They put the bicycle in a police van and drove me home. They said, 'Don't open your mouth and we'll ask your mother.' My mother told them she bought the bicycle at Walsh's Post Office. They said, 'He went to sell it, you know.' She said, 'Yes, he wants a motorbike.'

From then on I always used to be buying second-hand motor-cycles. My mother helped me. My mother thought the world of me, my darling mother. I dedicate this book to my mother. I bought a Rudge-Multi, belt driven. Them days you didn't do a test. You just needed a licence. You got on a motorbike and if you got killed it was your own fault. I'd no insurance and got away with it for years and years and years. Now this machine weighed over two hundredweight and on a wet day you couldn't get no speed because the belt was skidding. I went up to Hebden Bridge, Hardcastle Craggs, and while about four miles from Todmorden, the bike did a skid so I decided to over-haul it. It was a two-cylinder, two stroke, five and a half horse power with Lodge sparking plugs. I wanted to take it up to my bedroom. My mother said, 'You can't get it up these steep stairs.' So I thought, 'The next best thing is to take the bedroom window out.' So what I did, I took the machine to pieces out-side with some of the local boys and they tied a rope round them and I pulled them up to the bedroom window. I got the frame in. I got the petrol tank in. Then I got the engine in. I lifted this big rusty heavy engine in and I thought, 'I'm going to give this a good cleaning with a wire brush and paraffin oil.' Now then, I got the machine in the bedroom and spent months on it. I cleaned the cylinders. I took the pistons out. I cleaned the engine. And when I put it all togther my father come upstairs. He said, 'I'll have no more of this. The whole house smells of petrol. And you're smoking your pipe. You'll set the house on fire.' So I got the machine on its stand in the bedroom and kicked down the starter. Brrrrr. It run beautiful. Oh, it was lovely. It was a brand new machine. Then my father said, 'I want to ask you something. How are you going to get this machine out of the bedroom?!' and I'd to take it to pieces all over again!

I got other bikes as well. I had an India Super Chief, an American policeman's bike. It was ten horse power, belt driven, and had rocking-chair handlebars and a red petrol tank with a Sioux Indian's head on with all the feathers. I felt like a fly when I got on it. I got it for nine or ten pounds in working order. I'd the biggest motorbike in Manchester. I also had a Baby Levis. If you never had a Baby Levis in them days you wasn't with it. But I went mainly for the big machines—Harley Davidson, Francis Barnett 'Cruiser', Beardmore Precision. They cost me a bomb of money for petrol, 2/2d a gallon in them days. Most of my friends had motorbikes so I said to myself, 'Why shouldn't I have one? Why should I be poor? I'm doing menial jobs. I deserve it.' I used to get them on the never-never, or 'on the Bible' as they called it then.

I went up to the Summit once in a racing car, a Bugatti. My mother paid £19 for it. I'd no licence, no insurance, nothing. The first car I learned to drive was a tramcar—at Hydro Depot. Later on, in the 'thirties, I learned how to drive a bus at Princes Road Depot. They taught me how to skid. The place was greasy, full of oil. They'd spray a hosepipe on it. We used to go at full speed and skid round. Most passengers throw away their tickets in a bus, so the guards had a trick. They didn't punch the tickets and they used to pick up the clean ones, shave the ends off with a razor-blade and give them in as new. They'd have to be careful how they made their waybills out at the points. Inspectors jumped on to see if they could catch you. They came on not to examine the passengers' tickets but to see if you were frauding the Manchester Corporation.

While I was still on the trams I used to go to the front row of the Empire almost every night because I got a free ticket off my auntie who had five houses in Turkey Lane and took in the artistes, including the Tiller Girls, as lodgers. I got the Tiller Girls flowers cheap from Queen's Park Cemetery. When the bodies were buried and the relatives were gone, the diggers filling in the graves used to get the fresh and clean flowers and throw them up against the wall. I used to go and collect lovely big mixed bunches for my mother and the Tiller Girls. The Tiller Girls at the Empire all knew me. One night I'd have a bouquet of flowers for one of them and another night I'd have a bouquet of flowers for the next. Before the curtain come down I used to go up the stairs on to the stage with a nice black suit on and a white linen shirt and a starched collar and a black bow and, while the people clapped, I used to give a Girl, with the manager standing there, a nice bunch of flowers wrapped in tissue paper. I put my heart and soul in them flowers. I said, 'Thank you very much,' and then stepped down. Sometimes I used to stand by the orchestra and the leader used to hand the flowers to the manager to give. But the audience didn't know I used to take two or three Girls home every night to our house for a cup of tea. I didn't have no sex with them. I didn't want it. They didn't want it. They had boy friends of their own. I just kissed them and played with them, that's as far as it went. When I took them home they still had their warpaint on—all their lipstick and black eyebrow and mascara. They smelt beautiful. We used to get on top of a tram right from Turkey Lane down to No. 9, Pexton Street and I used to take them all a cup of tea. Then my mother said, 'I'll leave you now. You want to be on your own. But don't go to bed too late.' And she used to leave me in the kitchen with the Girls. They were all six foot nearly. They wore silk dresses and a kind of showy scarf that was all feathers. And some of them had priceless fur coats. They were all lovely girls, the pick, yet they were only getting £3-10 a week. They knew me as Sid. I'd put my arms round them while my old man and woman was in bed in the parlour. They pleased me and I pleased them and at twelve o'clock I used to see them all back to their digs in Turkey Lane. But they never knew from that day to this that I got the flowers from the cemetery.

After the trams I got a job in the bakehouse making biscuits at Crumpsall Biscuit Works, and this I thought was a steady job. I was in charge of feeding the ovens. We made cream crackers, Marie biscuits, Garibaldi, cream puffs, sultana puffs, petits beurres and zoological biscuits in the shape of little animals. Mornay Davis, the foreman, had beautiful muscles. Sometimes he let us go round the back hall and have a smoke while the cutters were being changed for another type of biscuit.

We had a white coat called a slop with CWS on. I'd put my own coat on over that and go round when it was coming towards five o'clock filling my trousers pockets and slop pockets and overcoat pockets off the trays at the back. I've gone down Charleston Road loaded with pounds of biscuits, beautiful fresh biscuits. One day one of the boys dropped some biscuits on Charleston Road and they put a watch on us and caught several and sacked them. Mr Charlton, who was over the essence department for giving taste, called us in to the dining-room and said, 'You can eat as many biscuits as you want while you work here, but there's no thieving. Anyone caught taking biscuits home will be sacked immediately.' But the thieving went on for ever. Come Friday night they used to sell us a big paper bag with mixed broken biscuits in. They sold us these at 6d a packet. We had to go up on Thursday, pay our sixpence to Mr Charlton and the biscuits were brought down on a truck on Friday.

I loved snakes. The girls in the packing room, packing biscuits, when they used to see me they said, 'There's the snake man! Oh, go away! Go away! You've got some snakes in your pocket!' And I said, 'Look at this beauty!' and the snake was about two and a half feet long, an ordinary grass snake, and I told them always, 'Get hold of it!' and the snake used to wriggle and all the girls run out. Once Mr Charlton caught me. He was very surly. He was a Scotchman, a miserable man. He said, 'Pick that snake up!' I picked the snake up and I said, 'Look! It's harmless!' and I rubbed it against his face. He said, 'Go into my office!' I went into his office and he said to me, 'Why do you bring those things to work? The girls are frightened. You're stopping production. The girls are running away from the benches. There are biscuits all over the floor.' I said. 'Look, it's only a lark. It's a bit of fun. These are grass snakes.'

I was sent home from work for two days, three days, many a time for bringing snakes. I kept them at home in the cistern. My father found out. He said to my sister, 'Win! Come up these stairs and have a look at this! He's put two snakes in the water swimming round and we've got to drink it! He's got to get rid of all them snakes. Otherwise he's got to go from here.'

I met a girl in the packing room called Irene Fletcher. She used to say to the other girls, 'The snakes he brings aren't poisonous. They won't kill you.' To give her justice she was a very attractive girl, plump built, round faced, and she had big blue eyes, blue and a piece of green mixed. I thought I was madly in love with her. I went out with her very very steady, courting. I used to take her every night up Charleston Road to her home in Harpurhey where the baths was. Everybody at Crumpsall Biscuit Works said, 'You're lucky, Rodge! I don't see what she sees in you. Doesn't she get scared of you? Apart from the snakes you're always doing weightlifting.' I said, 'Don't be stupid! I only do weightlifting by correspondence!'

Irene lived with her mother, a big stout woman that worked at the CWS eiderdown factory near Balloon Street, pumping feathers into eiderdowns. She was a domineering type. I was a bit scared when she first told me to come into the house. She said, 'If you want to see my daughter you'd better sit in the parlour with her, but only when I'm here.' The mother was in the kitchen with her own lover, a commercial traveller. He was suffering from Bright's disease. He was very pale in the face. His name was Mr Sanders. Mr Sanders, he came up every night. He never had a car. He came by bus or tram.

So I sat in the parlour every night with Irene. We hadn't much money to go to the pictures, though sometimes we went to the Prince's in Conran Street, second house. We sat on the sofa and, naturally, in time to come, the girl turned round at work and told me she was in trouble. I said, 'What kind of trouble are you in?' She said, 'I'm pregnant.' I said, 'Well, it's your mother's fault for letting me come in the house and sit in the parlour on the couch. I didn't like to do that to you. I

45

can't do nothing about it. I'll have to tell my mother and my father.'

When I told my mother and my father, my father gave me a black eye, he knocked me about. I retaliated: I set the lace curtains on fire and run out of the house. My mother went down to Willert Street Police Station across the road. The police was looking all over Collyhurst for me. That night I slept in Jimmy Bowles's house, a friend of mine who worked at the biscuit works. He said, 'I'll tell you where you can sleep. Sleep in our hen house and my mother and father won't know.' So I slept in the hen house with a lot of Rhode Island Reds. I was laid in the bottom of the hen house. Some of the hens had red mite and were doing their excreta on me. I slept in the hen house till next morning.

I went to work with hen muck all over me, not washed. Then I went home. My mother said, 'Where was you last night?' I said, 'I was sleeping at Jimmy Bowles's in the chicken house.' Before I knew where I was two policemen walked in and said, 'Come on, Sid. We're taking you to the station. Be quiet, now. Don't make no trouble because your father, you know, is a respectable citizen, he's a commissionaire. We respect your family.' They took me across to the police station where there was an ambulance waiting which took me to Crumpsall Hospital. My mother thought I wanted some treatment. Her idea was to put me away so that I wouldn't marry Irene Fletcher.

When I'd been in hospital a week my mother come to see me with some fruit and biscuits. Then this Mr Sanders come with a solicitor. He said to me in front of the solicitor and the sister and two nurses, 'There's nothing wrong with you. You can come out now and get married to Irene.'

I went to live at Irene's house for two or three days while the banns were put up. Mrs Fletcher, the mother, paid for the wedding, a quiet ceremony, no guests, in Christ Church, Harpurhey, and then I went back to Mrs Fletcher's. The irony of this story is that in front of Christ Church now stands a Maltese cross of pure white Italian marble and under that cross

46

lie my father, my eldest brother George, my sister Elizabeth and my brother Fred.

My brother Tom, he come up to the door one night and knocked on it and said, 'Your mother has found your place empty at Crumpsall Hospital. Listen, Sid. You've made your bed, lie on it. You've come out of hospital against Mother's wishes and married this girl. Don't ever come to Pexton Street again!'

The baby was born. It was a girl, christened Louise but we called her Lulu. I made her a lovely cot—she'd be about forty years of age now—but then I just drifted away from the house and Irene got a maintenance order against me, seventeen shillings and threepence a week, at Minshull Street Police Court. She was always throwing Jim from Connolly's Wire Works in my face when we had a little tiff. She had been going with him while she was courting me. Then I found out she was a prostitute. She and a girl called German Alice was on the beat together and going in Lewis's Arcade, Market Street. I went home and when I told them all about it my mother and father forgave me.

Several times I went down the town looking for my wife. I said, 'What are you doing with Lulu?' She said, 'My mother's minding her.' I said, 'Does your mother know you're on the town?' She said, 'Look, Sid, if it's the seventeen and three you're worrying about, I don't want no more money off you. I can earn five pounds easy in a day. My friend has her own car and we take clients to her house.' I said, 'I want to see the baby.' She said, 'I'm afraid you can't. My mother won't have you near the door.' I said, 'I'm leaving you for good!'

My mother and my father advised me to get away to Australia, to leave the country. My mother booked a passage for me on a steamship from Liverpool and gave me forty pounds. She came aboard the ship and about two hours before the ship sailed she said bye-bye to me and I can see her now put a handkerchief to her eyes, crying. I pretended to go into my cabin and I give her half an hour and then I went ashore myself

47

to miss the boat. I'd changed my mind. I thought, 'Why should I be pushed off to Australia because of a wife that's not worth it?!'

After three days I took a bus home. She was very surprised, my mother. She said, 'I thought you was on your way to Australia!' I said, 'Leave me alone! I'll tell you something. Whether you like it or not I've decided I want to be a sailor! I'm stopping at home for a day or two and then I'm going to sea.'

The Seas

My father knew Mr Shaw, the landlord of the Pineapple Inn. He'd two sons at sea on the Manchester Liners. One was a first mate and the second one, Arthur, was a chief steward. Arthur gave me a reference. I hung around Clara Street, that was where the Shipping Federation was. There was a strike on at the time. The two union men, Arthur Tipton and Jack Bolas, had gone to Liverpool to speak. Jack Bolas, a fat little chap, got thrown into the dock by men that was unemployed. I went to Mr Bolas when he come back, spoke to him nicely with the reference in my hand, and he got me a job as a cabin boy on the *Manchester Producer* of Manchester Liners Limited, Deansgate. I was disgusted because I was twenty-one and most cabin boys were fifteen or sixteen. I got four pounds a month and I had to pay ten shillings a month out of that, union money.

The *Manchester Producer* was the first ship I ever went on and it went to Canada. My job was to look after the passengers and the first, second and third mate and the skipper, the old man. The cargo over was cheese and Carnation milk. We brought back live cattle. Sometimes the poor cattle fell in the pens. The ship rolled at forty-five degrees when we got into the Western Ocean and there were swells forty feet high. We went what they call north-about, across the Great Western Ocean, that's the North Atlantic. We kept off the shipping lanes like the Cunard routes because of the fog round Labrador and round Newfoundland. We went to Nova Scotia and saw the fishing fleet on the Grand

49

Banks with all brown sails and big black numbers on them. Then there was a big sign on the quay—YOU ARE NOW ENTERING CANADA—at the beginning of the River St Lawrence and when we went in the River St Lawrence we stopped at Quebec. The men said, 'Don't go ashore, Rodge! Save yourself for the Indian squaw in Montreal!' but I went ashore. I saw all flares burning and these flares were big oil drums and on the top of the oil drums was like small canisters with lights, and there was hundreds of people ice-skating on a big lake. The first time I put my feet on the lake I fell flying on the cold ice.

I look back now to when I was a cabin boy. I used to cry because, four o'clock in the morning, all round my lips was yellow stuff with being sick. I saw several Cunarders at sea all lit up with beautiful lights. The ballrooms were lit up and all the portholes were lit up and it was a beautiful sight at twelve o'clock at night to see a ship three miles away from you and imagine the grand pianos going, the orchestra going, all the guests dancing in the ballroom. And there was I on a cattle and general cargo ship all the time sick, all the time sick! I went to bed three days with my Wellingtons on and my uniform suit on. I couldn't take them off, I never washed myself for three days, I was so sick. Then all of a sudden it came off me. I found the secret of seasickness. Eat dry Quaker Oats and you get yourself right again.

A lot of young people today want to go to sea. My advice is, leave the sea alone unless you go through a sea school. If I was going to sea again I would go on the *Arethusa* on the Medway up in Kent, I'd go on a training ship and become an officer, but I wouldn't go to sea as an ordinary common seaman or as a cabin boy or a steward. Even on the big ocean liners today there's a lot of jealousy amongst the stewards and squabbling and falling out over tips and I hate arguments with anybody.

At four o'clock in the morning I used to fill the teapot in the pantry with three spoonfuls of tea and sugar. If they wanted cocoa they'd to let me know the night before. I brought the bread to the galley and there I'd draw the fire and make two slices of toast and boil the kettle. Back in the pantry I scraped the toast and buttered it, made the tea and poured out a pint mug. I put a saucer over the mug and put the two slices of toast between two plates and put them all in a cloth and tied a knot and went along the side of the ship where the wind wasn't blowing. If the ship was rolling forty-five degrees I'd put my foot in the nearest scuppers and hold on like hell to an angle-iron. I went up three flights of stairs in the blackness. The only lights on the ship was the light on the masthead and the red light and the green light, the port and starboard lights, and, I tell you, you could see the white crests of the waves. It was a terrible sight. I found my way past the second deck where the Sparks, the wireless operator, was, and went up on to the bridge. I'd say, 'Good morning, sir,' to the officer on watch. He would say, 'Good morning, boy,' and I used to say, 'Here's your tea and here's your toast.' He'd say, 'Everything all right?' I'd say, 'Yes, sir. Everything's all right down below.' Then I used to go down below deck in the pantry and have a pint of tea myself after banking the fire up in the galley.

In the mornings I was up four o'clock. Bob Storey —he was the chief steward and what a chief steward!— he wasn't up then, he was still in his bunk. He was my boss. He never did no work. He was a giant of a man, about nineteen stone, and he used to stand against the lead sink in the pantry with his two thumbs in his belt and say, 'Boy, come here! Go down below and bring so and so out of the refrigerator!' and I had to pull the door up in the floor with a big iron ring and go down a staircase and bring up bacon, eggs, lettuce, meat, flour, potatoes, everything to be cooked.

When breakfast was served I used to go outside the saloon door and ring a big bell. Ding-a-ling-a-ling-a-ling-a-ling. That was eight o'clock, breakfast ready for all the officers except the one on the bridge and the one in the boiler room who had breakfast at about a quarter to nine. The skipper used to sit at the end of the table.

When I made the beds I used to look at the photographs of the officers' wives and children and at the revolvers. Under the pillows of each of the officers was a .45 Webley and Scott in case the crew mutinied. I placed the revolvers on the desk while I put the pillows straight.

At lunch time I used to take all the vegetables down to the galley and look after the cook. He'd say, 'Would you like a cup of tea, Rodge?' I'd say, 'Yes.' He always had the kettle boiling. Then we had our lunch in the pantry after all the officers was served. Chips, the carpenter, but not the Sparks, had his lunch with us. We washed up in the greasy deep lead sink. I made the water hot by turning the steam on from the steam pipe which made a terrible noise. Before you knew where you was the water was red hot. There was no hot water pipes, just cold water and steam.

The rest of the day I chipped ice off the brass portholes in the alleyway and put new Brasso on, which was unnecessary. I said to the chief steward, 'Why don't they paint these portholes instead of using Brasso? My hands are all cracked with chaps.' I also had to shake the mats over the rail. I've lost four door mats blown out of my hand into the Atlantic, and a gale force wind blew away a fourteen foot carpet belonging to a corridor.

At seven we dined in the fo'c's'le, the officers in the lounge in comfort. They had lovely carpets, a lovely small billiard table, a big dining table for fifteen, and a beautiful upright piano. I played the piano many a time when they weren't there. I played 'It's a Long Way to Tipperary', 'Pack up Your Troubles in Your Old Kit Bag', Schubert's 'Serenade', Liszt's 'Liebestraum', little pieces by Mozart and 'That Dear Old Fashioned Mother of Mine'. 'That Dear Old Fashioned Mother of Mine' was my mother's favourite. When I went home she used to say, 'Sid, play the piano. Play "That Dear Old Fashioned Mother of Mine".'

I went to bed at eleven. First the night wireless operator used to come down to me and say, 'Don't forget my shaving water,' and I used to take his shaving water up to his cabin on the second deck and then bring it back, wash out the mug and shaving tackle and take it back to his cabin again.

Sundays were dull. The cook baked the bread and all the crew washed their jeans and bits and pieces and hung them up aft on clothes lines. There was lifeboat practice too because of the fogs around Newfoundland Banks and Labrador. Sometimes we went for four days with the foghorn giving two blasts every five or six seconds. We couldn't see more than twenty yards in front of us. I used to bath myself at the back of the ship near the rudderchains. I stripped myself naked and let the bucket down with a rope and pulled it up with the salt water in it. At the finish I found out it was better to use the pump, midships. The pump water was de-salted and you could get a lather. If anybody tries to get a lather with salt water it's impossible.

We stayed in Montreal for four days loading cattle. When we landed I went into the galley with a big aluminium teapot to make tea for the officers. 'Are you going ashore tonight, Rodge?' someone said. 'No, what would I go ashore for?' I said. 'It's too cold and I haven't got much money.' 'But what about the Indian squaw?' 'The Indian squaw? Is it true?' I said. 'Yes, it's true. She lives on her own. She's only young. She's a thoroughbred Sioux Indian.' So I said, 'Tell me where she lives,' but they wouldn't say so I had to ask a policeman at the gate.

I took a pillowslip, about a pound of cheese, a tin of milk; I took some eggs; I took all sorts from the pantry. Bob Storey was already ashore or else I wouldn't have done it. He wouldn't have allowed me. He was a retired prison officer. I went ashore. I knocked at the door of this wooden hut and, who should come, but a beautiful Indian squaw. She was dressed in leather, rough brown leather, and all there was in this log cabin was no chairs, no furniture, just a big iron stove in the middle where she was burning logs. It was lovely and warm inside. She asked me to come in saying what did I want, in English. She spoke English

53

very well. I said, 'I've brought you some food to eat. The men told me about you.' She said, 'Take no notice of the men. There's a lot of men come here. I've to get the police to keep them away.' I said, 'Have you got a bedroom?' and, behind some sacking, there was this wide bed and it had no proper bedding on it, just rags. I said, 'What do you do for a living?' She said, 'I work at the Red Rose Tea Company. I might as well make you a cup of tea now you're here.' While she was making the cup of tea I was telling her all about Manchester. She said, 'What are you doing now?' I said, 'It's my first trip as a cabin boy.' And, to cut a long story short, she told me not to be shy, and I fell passionately in love with her that first night.

I came back six o'clock next morning and the first thing I did was went in the galley, lit the fires, got the cooks up and put the kettles and the pans on of hot water. I was a bit late and the officer that had been on the watch said, 'You were a bit late this morning, boy!' I said, 'Yes, sir. I've been ashore and I stopped with an Indian girl.' He said, 'I heard all about that. Don't let the men lead you on because she's a bit older than you.' I said, 'She's not older than me and she's very nice.'

During the journey home to Manchester, No. 7 Dock, Bob Storey told me, do this, do that. I said, 'Don't keep picking at me! I'm only getting four pound a month!' One day in the pantry he was cutting the meat up for dinner and the ship was rolling with a big swell and he held up a big piece of pork on the end of a big fork, he held it in front of my face because he knew I liked India and so I swore at him. He put the pork down on the board on the sink and he hit me right in the face. My eye all swelled up and I got a black eye. I went to the first mate and reported it. The first mate said he'd have a word with him and when we got to Salford Docks, after getting the cattle off at Mode Wheel Lock to be slaughtered in the abattoir, some of the crew told me that Bob Storey, chief steward, was going to get the sack for giving me this black eye. When he went

54

for his money he was called into the Shipping Federation and they give him his ticket there and then. I'd the union behind me. I'd an officer behind me. The officer who was behind me was minus a finger. He lost it on the *Manchester Commerce* when the *Voluma*, a Norwegian ship, went down with forty-two men in the Atlantic. Launching a lifeboat, he got his fingers tangled in a rope and it pulled his finger off. Another officer took the wedding ring off the finger and put it on another one. Today he's Captain Downing on the Manchester Liners.

I went home to Pexton Street. Now on the *Manchester Producer* was a Norwegian seaman. In his spare time in the afternoon he sat on the deck and he tattooed my arms. He only charged me seven and six for three tattooes. I've had them all these years, ever since I went to sea. On my arm I've got a Mercantile Marine Star and I've got Achensmith, the Russian strong man. On my right arm I have the Admiralty Anchor. Anyway, I was washing in the scullery at Pexton Street when my father come in and he saw my tattooes. When I'd got washed and dressed and tidy to go out he said, 'I want to talk to you a minute. How long have you had them tattooes on?' He was frantic. He said if I did anything wrong the police could always find me. But the best part of this was on his legs he himself had palm trees with snakes climbing up and there was daggers on his arms and a lion on his chest.

I transferred to the *Manchester Commerce*. There I was given a berth, as second steward this time, for eight pounds a month. That was a little better, and the chief steward was a gentleman. I passed the doctor. All he said was, 'Drop your trousers.' He only wanted to see if I'd VD. If you'd VD you wasn't allowed on the ship. You had to go to hospital. VD was very common amongst the seamen in them days. He never looked at your chest. He never looked at your eyes. He never looked anywhere else, only said, 'Drop your trousers,' and got hold of you with a piece of cane and said, 'You're OK,' and give you a certificate. You got it endorsed and got your advance note for two pounds eighteen to go to the ships' chandlers to buy some new socks and singlet and shorts. With two pounds eighteen you could buy a lot of stuff.

Whenever we were in Montreal I had the Indian squaw. I would go to the dock gates and past the policeman with his black bearskin hat on and his big black bearskin coat and his belt round him with a revolver. I ran to the cabin and she was waiting for me and when I knocked she opened the door. I always got scared going in, but once I was in I was all right. I said, 'Will you make me a cup of tea?' and we had a cup of tea together. We were madly in love, me and this Indian girl, madly in love.

Back in Manchester I seldom went home. I slept in the cranes and on the grain barges in Salford Docks. I stayed once at the Salvation Army in Ancoats Lane. You had to stay in two days working without pay. I was handed blocks six inches long to split into firewood and make bundles with wire round. These were taken in a Salvation Army van and sold to shopkeepers for three halfpence a bundle. I went once to the head man and said, 'I want to go out tonight.' He said, 'You can't go out tonight. You've got to work here two days.' So they kept me in working for two days chopping firewood, my hands was sore. And the food they give me, well I've seen chickens get better. The Salvation Army doesn't give you nothing. That's why they're millionaires today.

Two sorts of ship sailed out of the docks—the Princes Line with a white fleur de lys on the funnel and the Manchester Liners which had a red funnel with a black band. The Manchester Liners used to call at Partington Dock, take coal all night and leave in the morning. It was lovely to smell the smoke coming out of the funnels and to see the swell. One minute we'd be right up in the sky, the sea would be right down below, and the next it would be forty-five feet high and there was only the masthead showing. The Atlantic is very very rough. The last ship I went on was the *Manchester Division*. It took us fourteen days to Canada. On the way a very serious seaman, he was an able seaman, he says to me, 'Rodge, I want to tell you something when you're on your own. Come down to the fo'c's'le and I'll tell you something that will surprise you.' We went down and he said, 'There's a lot of talk about you in Salford in the pubs that you're going out with an Indian squaw. Even all the officers and the skipper know you're sleeping with her.' I said, 'Well, what of it? It's my own life. Are you jealous of me? Do you want the girl?' He said, 'Believe me, Rodge. I'm your friend. She's married to an officer on the CPL (The Canadian Pacific Line)'. I said, 'Well, why the devil doesn't he keep her better?! She's only got the clothes she stands up in. She has no furniture. Nothing.' He said, 'That's the way the squaws live. She'd be living in a wigwam not a wooden bungalow but for him.'

When we got to Montreal I saw the squaw waiting for me on the quayside. I didn't want to cause trouble between man and wife so I said to the men, 'Tell her I never come on this ship.' One man shouted this over the side of the rail while the dockers were getting all their tackle ready to unload the cargo. He shouted, 'Rodge isn't coming ashore! He's not on this ship! He's gone on another line!' She walked out of the docks and that was the last I saw of her.

Luckily when we come back to Manchester again and unloaded, I met a qualified seaman named John Ritchie who was to become my greatest friend. He was a handsome looking man, six foot. He'd been a weightlifter and a boxer. He could lift up a piano on his own, he was so strong. His father was an Australian, a retired captain, and kept a tobacconist's shop in Liverpool. I met him in the Salford Docks when we was both looking for another ship. He said to me, 'Haven't I seen you at the Shipping Federation?' I said, 'Yes. I'm a second steward. I'm looking for a ship. Can I come with you?' He said, 'OK. Let's go in the dry docks. There's a ship that'll be coming out tomorrow and we might be able to sign on her.' When the first mate said they'd got a full crew John said, 'Don't get disheartened. What we'll do, we'll get a lift in a lorry and we'll go to Liverpool.' So from the docks we got a lift in a lorry and went to Liverpool. We went right down to the pierhead at Liverpool where the Cunarders tie up. We could see New Brighton across the Mersey, and Wallasey. We saw the ferry coming and going. We saw Cammell Laird shipyard at Birkenhead and we saw the Royal Liver Buildings with the Liver Bird on top. And we saw Cooper's, the coffee grinders. You could smell the coffee as you come down the main street. For two nights we slept free of charge in the chefs' quarters of the biggest hotel in Liverpool, the Adelphi. A chef smuggled us in and John and the chef played cards. Then we walked aboard a tramp steamer taking general cargo and tramping for fourteen months. John went in the engineers' department and I signed on as a second steward.

We landed in New York. I said to John, 'How about us staying?' He said, 'You want us to jump the ship?' I said, 'Yes. Let's see if we can get a job in America. There's not much doing in Manchester and there's not much doing in Liverpool.' I didn't want to go while I was waiting for a ship to Albion Street Labour Exchange and queue up for the dole which was only seventeen and threepence, and I didn't want to go as a docker sitting in the compound all day on fifteen shillings a day waiting for ships to unload. He said, 'OK. We'll jump the ship. We can always work our passage back as DBS (Discharged British Seaman).' So we jumped this ship in New York.

We took jobs in restaurants and cafés. John was taking jobs as a cook and I was peeling potatoes with a machine, turning the handle round, and selling ice-cream. And there was a man if you stood up to him you got five dollars. I went in the ring and I come out full of blood but I got my five dollars. In Baltimore I did the same thing. I got up against a professional. I got a few good punches in and knocked him in the corner, but he came out of the corner like a wild bull and chased me round the ring and pummelled me up. My face was red with blood and his gloves were saturated with blood and they wanted to call off the fight but I said, 'No, no, no! Carry on! I'm only here for five minutes!' I wanted the money badly. I stood there for five minutes being pummelled up. In the dressing-room they allowed me to have a shower. John said, 'You didn't half look a sight when you came out of the ring! How much did they give you?' I said, 'Seven dollars.' All we wanted to do was live and survive and get some money. In England there were millions out of work, the mines closing down, the cotton mills closing down and leaving the machinery behind, beautiful machinery, and bales of cotton. Men were queuing up for bowls of pea soup and they only got seventeen and three a week and had to wait for hours to get it and were treated like cattle. They were dressed in big hobnailed boots, dirty tweed jacket and trousers. They had a muffler round their neck and a cap on them. They were uncouth and unshaven. They were swearing and spitting and smoking Willies and Players Weights. Thousands were stood at street corners doing nothing.

America was dry, on prohibition, but John and me didn't care. We knew where we could get liquor if we wanted it because seamen told each other, you can go to such a house and such a house, or such a shop and such a shop, and they'd take you to the back and you could drink to your heart's content with tough characters, mostly seamen and foreigners. I didn't bother with the bootleg liquor racket but John liked a drink so I used to go in these dives with him now and again. I'd have a couple of drinks and that was about all. It was firewater. There was a gangster at the time called Dutch Schultz, the Beer Baron of the Bronx. With three more hoodlums he was trailing some lorries loaded with illicit liquor. He was trying to kill the drivers and get the liquor to his warehouse. But the FBI caught up with him, got level with his car, opened two windows and killed every man in the car. The car run off the road on to the grass verge . . .

I must tell about Legs Diamond . . . I was stood with John in front of a theatre in New York. John was getting some cigarettes and a man in plain clothes said to us would we kindly remove ourselves away from this spot as there was going to be a killing done. I got alarmed. I said to John, 'Come on!'

But one of the men said, 'It's all right. We're police officers. There'll be a woman coming out and a man coming out and the man will be shot. So keep away in case you get hurt.' Inside that theatre was Jack Legs Diamond, the big gangster. They'd been looking for him for months—for killings, hi-jackings . . . He had a string of brothels. He was in every racket. The Mafia was tame to this.

Well, he came out of the theatre, Jack Diamond. We stood on the other side of the road and, I saw with my own two eyes, Jack Diamond come out of the theatre with a lady in a red coat. The lady asked him to stand there while she went to the tobacco kiosk to get some cigarettes. The next thing I saw him spin round twice. He'd been shot with sixteen rounds of sub-machine gun ammunition. They shot him dead. This lady grassed on him. She was one of his playmates but she grassed on him because he had about half a dozen women. She told the police she'd be at the theatre at a certain time and bring him out at a certain time, at three o'clock in the afternoon. And the FBI was waiting. They got him. They took his body off the pavement, put it in an ambulance, took it away, and there was nothing but bloodstains. The bullets went so fast out of these Thomson sub-machine guns, I seen him turn round twice before he did half a somersault and fell sprawled on the pavement, hands and legs full out. Everyone who stood round screamed when they saw his body. It turned my heart sick and I went away with John.

The next one on the list was Al Capone. That was after John and I had done odd jobs for about a year in New York, Boston, Philadelphia, Galveston, Houston in Texas, New York again, bumming, out of work, in jobs, out of jobs. The police at the time were trying to stop the hi-jacking of liquor at midnight on the roads, six or seven lorry-loads of liquor. They'd stop the lorries and get all the barrels of liquor thrown into the roadway and set the lorries on fire. The drivers was taken away to the police station and sent to prison in vans. That's how they caught Al Capone. Al Capone was the biggest of the lot. He

60

was sent to Alcatraz. I remember him going to Alcatraz prison and another prisoner stabbed him in the back with a pair of scissors . . .

A regular thing in them days was the funeral parlours. Top brass gangsters used to walk with a coffin. They'd open two doors and take the coffin and put it in a kind of sarcophagus. All of a sudden a bomb would go off, a bomb planted amongst the flowers, a time bomb, and a rival gang would rush the doors and open up with machine-guns. That's how a lot of gangsters got blown to pieces. It was mass murder. When John and me was in Boston men was putting new doors in where there'd been a bomb. We knew it had been gangster warfare. They were worse than the IRA.

There was a lady called Cigar-Smoking Moll. She carried two .38 Colts. She was a policeman killer. She was pulled up on the highway by a patrolman on a ten horsepower India Super Chief. She got out of her car and said, 'What's to do, officer?' She got her two revolvers out with a cigar in her mouth and she shot him dead. Then she got back in the car and run over his machine and left him.

One February seven men were stood with their chests to a garage wall by two rival gangsters with machine-guns. There was a devil of a noise and that was the St Valentine's Day Massacre . . .

John and I bummed in America for three years. Everything above board and honest. I never stole nothing. He never stole nothing. When we wasn't working we stood in soup queues an hour at a time for a bowl of soup. Day after day we had this soup.

Texas was very nice. You could always knock at a door and get a meal if you chopped wood, cleaned windows, did painting, did chores. People today look at Texas as a cowboy land. It is a cowboy land in a sense—there's millions of cattle out there. But there's also thousands of goats. In Texas they like goats.

We went to Florida to the Everglades. We were ankle deep in

grass and mud and some tourists said, 'You've got to get a boat. A man will take you for about eight dollars.' We knocked some money together and went with a chap for about half an hour. He said to John, 'If you hold the tiller I'll come with you and your pal as guest.' So we went in this boat for nothing down the Everglades and I've never seen a better sight—the water, marshes, long reeds, trees, riverbanks. Growing in the water was cypress trees. You can make a sideboard of this wood. It's very easy to work with a jack-plane. And there was every sort of bird—eagles, egrets—and every sort of animal— crocodiles, alligators, snakes. I'd like to see the Everglades again.

In Louisiana I had the finest bath I've ever had in my life. There was six baths all level with the floor—no tiles, nothing posh—and these baths were made of rough cement, you could put soap on the floor and you couldn't slip. All you had to do was walk down three steps and turn valves on the wall, a white valve for the cold water and a red valve for the hot steam, and within about twenty-five to thirty seconds the cold water was hot enough for a bath. We paid seventy-five cents and the baths held four times more than the public baths in England and they smelt sweet. All round the wall was a wooden seat and you could sit there with other men and just walk about nude like they do in Japan. I thought of the dirty small glazed baths in England where they'd got to keep on cleaning them out, cleaning them out, and bending down to scrub the scummy line. The plug holes in these baths had an iron thing over them about six inches across and you just pushed it down and the water went down in one big gulp. To clean the baths a man used a broom and steam and then cold water. John said to the attendant, 'I'm sorry I can't give you a tip. We're on the road, looking for a job. But I'll give you some cigarettes.'

We were walking along once and we come to a desert, all sand, very very hot. In Arizona that was. Beside the desert was a shanty town and a wooden house and a hilly-billy who said, 'Where are you going? It'll take you two days to get across there unless you've got a car.' So we had to turn back. That was the first time I saw a desert in America. There's another one with big red rocks.

In California I saw the tallest trees in the world, the redwoods, a hundred and twenty-five feet high some of them, some a hundred and thirty. There's been two seats put inside one of these redwoods and you can ride through it in a car. The Californian people are very friendly people. We just knocked on the door and told them politely that we wanted food and they called us inside and gave us a meal.

We stayed in Chicago for five or six months. John got a job in a meat-packing firm and I worked in a tailor's shop cleaning and sweeping up. We got digs together in a big red building. A lot of women in the building was loose women, bad women, but they never bothered with us because they knew we didn't have much money. I remember the black and white kids playing in the streets of Chicago. Never talk about the slums of London. Chicago is a darned sight worse.

While John and I was in Philadelphia I found out more about the protection racket. We went to the docks—we wasn't looking for a ship, we was looking for a meal—and I seen fistfuls of dollars changing hands between lorry drivers and a well-dressed man. I asked someone, I said, 'Who's this fellow, this well-dressed man? Do you think he could find me a job?' He said, 'Leave him alone! He's a hoodlum! He'd shoot you as fast as you could talk to him!' This well-dressed man was paying hundreds of dollars to the lorry drivers for the night's work they'd done.

America was full of criminals. Even some of the police were crooked, crooked as a corkscrew. I wanted to get back to Blighty. Not that England was much better. The estimate of the prison population there was thirty-six thousand people and they were still hanging them at Strangeways Jail, Manchester. I remember some of the IRA getting hung there; also Dr Ruxton, a brilliant Hindu doctor who cut his wife to pieces and then the maid in case she'd give the game away; also a

Yiddish boy who slept with a girl for the night and when she stole his money strangled her with her own stocking.

John and I returned to New York and signed as DBS on the *Bremen* which was sailing for Southampton in a few days' time. Now, in the harbour, was a beautiful millionairess with a big white yacht and a crew of about nine or ten. I met her on shore and she smiled at me and I smiled at her and we got talking. I said, 'What a beautiful yacht you've got!' and she says, 'Come aboard and have a look. You come from New England, don't you?' I says, 'No, I don't come from New England. I come from England. I'm on a ship across there anchored in the roads. I'm a steward.' So she invited me aboard this yacht. And what a beautiful yacht! It was a diesel yacht, all white with a green water-line and a big yellow funnel. 'Come down below!' she said and told one of the cooks to go to the galley and bring a meal. 'Wait here in the lounge,' she said. 'I'll be back in a few minutes.' The meal was brought— vegetables and steak. What a steak! Then the millionairess came back and gave me some whiskey and said, 'I rather like you.' I said, 'What a pity I'm already married to a woman in England and she's got a child and I can't afford a divorce!' She said, 'On what grounds would you get a divorce?' I said, 'To be honest with you, she's on the streets, a prostitute. But a divorce will mean a scandal and all that sort of thing. I suggest you meet our third mate. He's a very nice young man, about my age.'

I went back to the boat and told John. 'The millionairess wants me,' I says. John says, 'We're fixed up then.' I says, 'No. I'm arranging for her to meet the third mate.' John says, 'Are you crazy?!'

Well, all of a sudden the millionairess pulled alongside one afternoon at two o'clock and began flirting with the third mate. He went to his cabin saying, 'I won't be long, darling!' and came back carrying a hold-all. Meanwhile she was talking to me. I was bending over the rail of the ship. She said, 'Why don't you come and see me again?' and she told me her home address. I was very attracted to her, not because of her money, no, the reason why I liked this lady was she was straight out, she didn't flurry her words. Then the third mate come back and he went down the pilot ladder and boarded the yacht. She waved to me when they was about a hundred and fifty feet from the liner and John said to me, 'Sid, you're all right there! She still wants you!' But the irony of it is I forgot to put her address down. I kept thinking afterwards, 'Where did she say she lived? Where did she say she lived?' I'd forgot her address, absolutely forgot it.

Back in Manchester, John and I got a job as dockers. Mr Steele, the Superintendent of the Salford Docks at that period, said we could hang about in the Control. The Control was like a big cattle-pen and all the dockers that were waiting for a ship to come in and unload waited there day time and night time six hours. After the six hours they got fifteen shillings for waiting in the Control. It had a corrugated roof over it with bars all round. A man would come in. He'd say, 'I want seven men to unload a ship.' Probably it'd be barbed wire or little bags of graphite which were very slippy. It'd be cheese. It'd be general cargo. It could be anything. It could be sacks of potatoes from the continent, off what they called the weekly ships that fetched vegetables from Belgium and France. We unloaded all sorts, but the worst thing I ever unloaded in all my life was steel billets. We were sent to Partingdon. There was a ship tied up there and it was loaded with steel billets. Steel billets weighed nearly a hundredweight. It took two men to lift a steel billet up and you had to be very careful not to get your fingers trapped. Most of my fingers at the end were bleeding. These steel billets was rusty. We had to put them in the middle of the floor. The crane come down with a grab and we put them in the grab, about twenty billets in each grab, and the checker said, 'Right!' and the crane took the grab up and spewed them all out into railway trucks. There was two men on the quayside stacking them in railway trucks to take them to the iron foundry to be smelted down. We also shovelled up iron ore off the floor and put it in a grab. It was just like shovelling coal. Some was in big cobs and some was in small cobs. We was smothered in iron ore dust. After eight hours down below you was glad to get out. It took us four days to unload a ship of iron ore, six days to unload a ship with iron billets on.

At last John says to me, 'Now look here, Sid,' he says, 'I've had enough of unloading bloody ships. I don't like this caper. Look at your hands! No more unloading ships! Mr Steele can do what he likes with himself because I'm not going on as a docker!' So John went his way and I went home and from that day to this I'm sorry to say I lost my pal. I've lost John. He's lost me. He doesn't know where I live. I don't know where he lives. He might be dead for all I know. He was a good boy, a good Englishman.

The family had moved from Pexton Street to the Plaza Dining Room at the corner of Alexander Street. It was a beautiful big shop downstairs and the rent was two pound seventeen and six a week. There were enamel bowls in the window and my mother had men come down from the Manchester Corporation and fit some gas pipes under the bowls. I had to go to Butler Street, a very rough area on Oldham Road, and get ribs for fourpence a pound. I used to get ten or twelve pound and put them in a small sack and my mother stewed them up and put lentils and barley in and made a lovely soup. Men used to come in—clean men, old men, disfigured men, bad men, good men—and they used to get a lovely big bowl of soup for threepence. One day an old man come in. He asked for an ounce of thick twist. He had two bowls of soup and he had some potato pie. He got up and he said to my mother, 'I've got no money to pay you, luv. What am I going to do?' My mother said, 'I know what I'm going to do. I'm going to get one of my sons. He's a big lad and he does a lot of wrestling.' And when I come in I got hold of the old man and said, 'Give that tobacco back and get outside or I'll bring the police!' He went outside the door, he took his boot off and he threw it right through the door-glass window. I run up the pavement and I grabbed hold of him and I give him a jolly good hiding and the police came and took him to the nick.

Soon after that I joined a dipping school run by the Royal Navy in Chatham. I'd to dive in a Siebe Gorman diving suit but the boots were too big for me, it took me all my time to pick my feet up under water. I'd to dive off a launch in a lock with an airline and a compressor working from the airline, and show how long a diver can keep down. I walked along the bottom of the lock in a foot of mud and came up the other side where the lock gates were. My mother got me out after six weeks. I didn't like the discipline. Instead I scraped and painted hulls at Portsmouth, Devonport, Rosyth and Scapa Flow.

One summer I answered an advertisement in the *Evening Chronicle*. Carlos' International Diving Circus wanted a diver at Southend-on-Sea. I'd never been to Southend in my life. I answered by telegram. They sent a telegram back. Carlos was an Englishman. His wife was a Russian. They asked me to dive off a platform seventy feet in the air into a tank. I did it twice, but I didn't like it because the tank wasn't big enough. When they asked me to do the fire dive in a sack of flames, I refused. So Carlos said, 'Sid, I'll tell you what. You're a very powerful swimmer and I've got the Britannia Pier, Great Yarmouth, booked for a diving display for the whole summer season. Would you like to take it over? We'll work on a percentage, you and I. You send me so much money every week.'

I went to Great Yarmouth. I saw the captain with his binoculars at the end of the pier and I was classed as 'Brahma the High Diver'. When the tide was out I had a twenty-five foot drop and when it was in I had a fifteen foot drop from the board. The currents were terrible. You could tear yourself to pieces on the pylons because they were covered with barnacles and shells. I got a lady from the Labour Exchange and dressed her up as a nurse to take round the box. A mile from the pier-head you could see Scroby Sand. Scroby Sand was full of seals, all lying asleep, basking in the sunshine. Many a time I swam to lie among them.

One day Ferranti's Works come. All of a sudden seven hundred people were there to see the diver and I said, 'Ladies and Gentlemen, would you kindly give the lady silver. Make it a silver collection.' And that day I made thirty pound with five dives—a swallow dive, backdropping dive, falling statue dive, side dive and jack-knife dive. The last dive the tide had gone well out. I was still diving into deep water but I'd a bigger drop. The water was very very cold and when I tried to make for the pylons to the Jacob's ladder, the pilot ladder, I found I couldn't make it, I was being washed out to sea. So I swam down with the cold current and pulled my way with my left arm to the beach. I was more scared than ever before in my life. It was a mile and a half to the beach. I laid on the sands amongst the people and they all clamoured round me. Then I walked in my swimming costume down the front, right along the promenade and got myself dressed under the pier in the little cabin where I always changed. People were clapping me.

One very hot day when the tide was at flood I got another good crowd so I said, 'Ladies and Gentlemen, will you kindly make it a silver collection as I'll be swimming amongst sharks.' There was a shoal of porpoises very near the pylons of the pier and these porpoises was diving in and out of the water. An old lady says, 'You can't dive in there now amongst all them sharks!' I said, 'Ladies and Gentlemen, sharks or no sharks, I've got to dive in. This is my bread and butter. I'll be out in two minutes to do my next dive.' One lady put a ten shilling note in and another lady put half a crown. When I opened the box it was full of notes and silver just because of the porpoises. I wish the porpoises had come every day!

In September I went to Lowestoft to see the fishing girls gutting the herrings and then I came home to Manchester. I was tired. I'd split two costumes right down the stomach with doing belly dives from slipping on the board. My legs were black and blue. Towards the end of the season the wind was howling

68

every time I got to the top of the board. I told the sea captain with his binoculars I was leaving and I said goodbye to the sea-lions on Scroby Sand. I had to spend three days in Manchester resting and rubbing my legs with Vaseline. Then I answered an advertisement of the Genoa Salvage Company. They wanted a relief diver and they paid my fare out. I was the only Englishman. All the rest were Italians.

First we did small wrecks not far from Belgium. We sailed out from Ushant to a marker buoy and brought up bronze propellers and copper piping and brass portholes. We used hydrogen cutters —you can't use acetylene under water. We wore Siebe Gorman and Neufeldt diving suits. Before I went down I had half a cupful of rum to give me false courage. If I went down to any big depth I used to come up and stop still, hanging by my line, for twenty-five minutes so as not to get the bends. When we come on deck we went straight into the decompressing chamber and the helmet and suit was taken off us and we'd to sit there for three hours to get back to normal. I've been more times in a decompressing chamber than I've had cups of tea. Deep-sea diving's not a pleasant job—I suffered from headaches and I lost a lot of weight. But there's one wreck I've always wanted to walk the deck of and that's the *Lusitania* which was torpedoed in 1915. She went down off a place in the South of Ireland called Kinsale. She's lying in one hundred and seventy feet of water, that's all, and in the baggage room is millions of pounds' worth of diamonds and gems.

After Ushant we worked on wrecks in the Indian Ocean. The floor of the Indian Ocean was beautiful and very very peaceful. I wasn't frightened of the sharks. I tickled their bellies. They didn't go for you direct, they went round you in circles and each time they went round they come closer and closer and you could let air-bubbles out of your helmet to scare them away. The most dangerous fish was the codfish. The codfish attacked your helmet and knocked you right off your feet. A manta ray, if you stood on him, only waved his flippers like a butterfly and threw you up in the water.

69

In the Indian Ocean we got three million pounds worth of rupees and silver out of the P and O liner *Egypt*. But we lost two divers. Four decks had to be blasted away and the charges went off before the divers could get off the ship. That's what made me give up the sea for good.

The Germans

I joined the 6th/7th Manchester Regiment, Territorials. I remember coming from Stretford Road Barracks to Worsley when King George V and Queen Mary was given a review. I shook hands with King George V and I seen Queen Mary in one of them big fine beautiful hats she used to wear. I sat up and sat down behind what they call a limber, driven by three big horses in single file. It carried an oven with a chimney. It had coal and I had to stoke up and make a stew and boil cabbage and boil potatoes going along a main road. By the time I landed at Worsley the food was cooked so I had to damper down the fire for the troops to have a meal. Then we got in formation to meet George V and Queen Mary.

I went to Diggle in Yorkshire nearly every weekend. I used to fire a Mark 3 Lee Enfield, that's a service rifle. We had all Saturday afternoon and Sunday to get sixty points but I never worked on the range on a Sunday, only in the butts putting the targets up and putting them down. Every Saturday by five o'clock when the sergeant blew his whistle I had my sixty points. I used to see lumps of grass and turf flying up in the air at a thousand yards. The others were firing down too low some of them, and some of them were firing too high. The secret with a weapon like a .303 is to take your first pressure and you don't take your second pressure till you've got the tip of your foresight level with the bottom of the V in the backsight, and then you aim. I used to fire no more than five rounds out of the ten but I got my sixty points by Saturday before five o'clock. I remem-

71

ber a Saturday at Diggle—all moors, miles round was moors—when we had to lay down on our stomachs in the snow. The sergeant was a big red-faced sergeant with a big moustache. 'Now you fellows,' he says, 'see if you can get your sixty points today. Rogers,' he says, 'take it easy!' I had three sessions of laying in the snow and I got my sixty points in. Monday night after being at Diggle if you got your sixty points you'd queue up in the drill hall at a green baize table and you'd salute an officer and there was ten shillings silver waiting for you. You'd say, 'Very good, sir!' salute, left turn and away.

I was in Headquarter Wing under Sergeant Scafe. I was a cook but I didn't have to cook except when we went to camp, fourteen days under canvas at Catterick, and then I was put on the peg mostly because I never used to like blancoing all my equipment. We wore puttees not just ordinary trousers in them days. I got told off many a time by the officers and sergeants. 'Your equipment's very greasy!' We had to do all the brassware, go over all our buttons with a button stick. Your big heavy army boots had to be blacked. We had to do what we called 'spit and shine.' I didn't like that. But I liked the smell of the gun cotton.

On a Friday night there used to be wrestling in the drill hall. As I was not a professional I got one pound win, ten shillings lose. One night I went up there to wrestle a coalminer. He was very well built but big as he was I beat him easily. The best known wrestlers in Manchester in them days was the Pye brothers.

When the Second World War broke out I was in charge of the armoury at the barracks, cleaning all the guns up—machine guns and everything, real stuff. I'd a kind of leather apron round me and I'd plenty of oil. Thick oil smelt like castor oil. I used to get the rifles down out of the racks, take the bolts out, pull-through the barrels. Even the stocks I'd to oil. There's not one man in London can tell more about the bolts and screws of a .303. My rifles have been over the top and fired. They take a big bullet, a big brass bullet that kills you.

I wanted to do my bit in the army but they wouldn't let me. I went down to Dover Street Recruiting Office. I waited there on a form and they called my name, 'Sidney Arthur Brahma Rogers, will you come this way please!' When I went I had a strict medical examination. I didn't want to get out, I wanted to go in the army or go in the convoys and fight the U-boat menace. But I got five red crosses in red ink on my card. I says, 'I'm all right, doctor!' He said, 'I'm afraid you're not. You've got a weak heart. You can't go to war but you can do ARP work.' I said, 'I don't want to do ARP work.'

I was living on my own in a furnished room at No 5, Raby Street, Worley Range, when the blitz started. I came home one night at seven o'clock. I could see sparks flying up because at Platt Fields was the ack-ack guns, and the sparks were flying up where the bits of lead were hitting the pavement. I remember I run under the stairs where all the guests of the house were collected.

A second night the sirens had been gone about an hour and the Germans were well over and I was on the pavement when I saw a German fighter overhead. He was well below the barrage balloons and he came over the roofs and he wouldn't be more than thirty feet above the roof of the house where I lived. I had the key in my hand, I had only about ten yards to go to the front door, and I saw the swastika on the plane and I saw the head of the pilot lean over to look at me—he'd a leather helmet with goggles on—and he opened up with a machine gun at me and all around me spattered machine gun bullets as he went right across Worley Range towards Stretford Road.

The Germans came over night after night bombing. Manchester was badly blitzed. I could hear the bombs and I could hear the flak falling on the cobblestones. Our house was blessed. Opposite was thirteen houses razed to the ground and twenty-one people killed while a wedding party was going on.

I was now on the buses at Princes Road Depot. Princes Road Depot was the best depot I ever worked in. All the buses used to get washed every night. One morning early I was half asleep. I had everything ready to take a bus out. I'd got my card and signed on and I went to the canteen for a cup of tea. We used to get a cup of tea for twopence and a bun for a penny. A conductress, a lovely curly-headed blonde about twenty-seven years of age, came over to me. She said, 'Hello, Sid.' I said, 'Hello. How's your husband going on?' I knew this lady. She did plenty of sewing when she was finished with a Singer sewing machine making lovely frocks. She said, 'I'm dying for a baby. My husband can't make one some way. Would you like to help me? When is your day off?' I told her. She said, 'I'll try and get off that day. You come down to my house in Baguley.' Well, I'd worked the Baguley route near Southern Cemetery, that's where Alcock and Browne's buried and on the grave they've got two crossed propellers. I says, 'I don't want to get involved because your husband seems a nice guy.' She said, 'He won't mind if he finds out.' I says, 'I'm very very sorry, I can't come down to the house but, I'll tell you what we can do, why not have a bus child?' There was about eighty buses in the depot five o'clock every morning. 'Come early in the morning.' She says, 'That's a good idea. I come at six anyway.' I says, 'Come about quarter to six. We'll go upstairs in a bus right in the corner of the shed and I'll try and see what I can do there.'

I took her upstairs and she put her bag down and we made love—call it 'love'?—and she got pregnant. Now her husband was very very friendly after this. He kept buying me cups of tea every morning. 'I know,' he said, 'and I'm very glad.' But there's a tragedy about this. While his wife was pregnant she had a quarrel with a passenger. The passenger, another woman, hit her and struggled with her and pushed her off the bus and she was laying there in the middle of the road with a miscarriage and they had to bring the ambulance.

One morning I was going to Platt Lane taking some people from Avro's factory, mostly women. You could smell the varnish on them from painting the plane wings a mile off. I was taking them off the night shift. I went round Bradford

Cemetery way and I got stuck under an iron bridge. The roof all crumpled in. The women were cursing me. 'Oh my God,' they were saying, 'what are we to do now?! Hang about this miserable place?!' I said, 'Yes. You've got to wait till we get a relief.' My mate had to get on a telephone and a big crane had to drag the bus out.

Another time I was driving a bus from Parrs Wood Depot to Piccadilly before the old Piccadilly Gardens was changed. When I was coming down Mosley Street the sirens started going. That was seven o'clock. I pulled the bus up alongside. An air-raid warden said to me, 'Driver, if I was you I'd get in the shelter under that warehouse. There'll be splinters flying all over the town.' So me and my mate went down under the warehouse and was there till four o'clock in the morning. The basement was reinforced specially with girders and concrete and there was about a hundred and fifty people with us. We could hear the bombs going off all round us while we was drinking tea. My mate says, 'Our bus I think will have it tonight!' I said, 'To hell with the bus! They've plenty of money, the Corporation. Why worry about the bus?! Have you got the takings?!' 'Yes,' he said. 'I've left the tickets but I've got the money.' 'Well, I said, 'that's all you've got to worry about.'

When we come out at four all Piccadilly, Manchester, was ablaze. I believe Coventry got it worse and London got it very bad. We saw our bus from about fifty yards and my mate said, 'Look at that, Sid! Not a window left but it's still standing!' The windows were broken not with bombs but with our own British ack-ack. As all the shells bursted in the sky all the pieces come down and shattered the glass and dented the roof. We looked all round. The floor inside was littered with glass and the floor upstairs was littered with glass. I switched the engine on. She was going perfectly. I said to my mate, 'I'll drive back slowly. Clear a seat and sit down,' and I drove the bus back slowly to Parrs Wood Depot.

Next I worked for the Carborundum Company making wheels for grinding torpedo heads, wheels for grinding shells,

75

wheels for grinding anything. The Carborundum Company is a Canadian firm and on the stones they have a label with an Indian Sioux's head on with all the war feathers. Carborundum wheels can run into hundreds of pounds. The finest grinding wheel in the world is the puddle wheel, three feet in diameter. One day the foreman came to me and he said, 'Sid, we're trying an experiment.' I puddled a brown dust up in a macerator and poured it into moulds, twelve moulds at a time, lined with grease-proof paper like you bake a cake. I tippled them up left and right, left and right, to get the air holes out of them, and when I got all the air holes out of them I put them in a rack and they was pushed in the kilns. They was a great success. I invented the puddle wheel.

One Sunday morning while at the Carborundum I went through Whitworth Park off Oxford Road with Ali Baba, my alsatian dog, and who should I see sat on a seat but a beautiful young woman. I smiled to her and she smiled to me so I said, 'It's a lovely day, isn't it?' She said, 'The *weather*'s very nice, yes.' I said, 'Excuse me asking you, but are you English?' She said, 'No, I'm German.' 'Oh,' I said, 'I see. I've been all over the world myself.' She said, 'Where do *you* come from?' I said, 'I come from India.' She looked at me. She didn't believe me with being white. She said she was going to the Holy Name Church in Ackers Street on Oxford Road. I said, 'You must be a Catholic then.' She said, 'Yes.' I said, 'Well, I'm a Church of England. I might as well be straight with you. But can I walk down with you? Can I see you to the church?' She said, 'I don't mind.' So I walked her down to the church, a five minutes' walk. She said, 'I must go across now. All the people are going into the church.' I said, 'Are you very religious?' She said, 'Oh yes. One of my brothers is a priest in Germany.' I said, 'Can I wait for you coming out?' She said, 'All right then. You wait for me.' I said, 'You won't come out of another door and do that sort of business?' She said, 'No. You wait for me.'

When she came out of the church I was very happy and Ali

76

Baba ran up and kissed her hand. I walked with her up to Platt Fields where the monument of Abraham Lincoln is, the man who's supposed to have freed the slaves in America, a beautiful big bronze statue about ten feet high. Then I walked with her to where she lived, a hostel belonging to the Society of Friends in Peter Street near the Midland Hotel. She said, 'They're very good to me, the Quakers.' I said, 'Are you happy there?' She said, 'Yes. That Mr Howard, the secretary, would give you anything—money, furniture, clothes. The Quakers, believe me, they are good people. They're very generous.' When I left her at the door of this hostel I asked her would she like to come and see a film that afternoon but I'd have to take my dog home first to my home in Worley Range. She said, 'Yes, I'd like to see a film,' so I took the dog home and I met her that afternoon. We went to see *Oliver Twist*. It was a gorgeous film and she enjoyed it and during the pictures I was holding her hands and this was something different to me. She told me she'd been interned for three years with six thousand women in Port Erin at the Bay Hotel on the Isle of Man. She was Category C (I don't know what that means), but through Mrs Keane, an interpreter from Scotland, she got let out because her uncle was a Reichsfinanzminister imprisoned by the Nazis.

We saw each other every evening. I was at the Carborundum and she was working as a cook in Sam's Chop House, Corporation Street. I introduced her to my mother who was taking in officer lodgers in Ruskin Road, Droylsden.

My mother was by now twice a widow but she was still a very attractive woman. She was very stout but she had a lovely waist on her, I could put my hands round her waist and make them both touch. She also had a lovely bosom on her and she used to wear lovely clothes. I remember one day after my father died I said, 'Mother, will you come out with me tonight and have a drink at the New Inn?' She put on a lovely dress and when we got inside there was an orchestra comprising of a violin, a cello and a piano. We sat next to it in the far corner and I bought her a Guinness and I had a small glass of beer. She was sat there in her dress and her fur coat and I couldn't help seeing her Divine of Love, that is the parting of the breasts. Hers were so beautiful you thought they'd been moulded out of clay. I said, 'How's your second courting days going on?' She was courting a gentleman that had fifteen garages and was supposed to be a teetotaller but I'd seen him several times come out of a public house and the landlord told me he was a secret whisky drinker. She said, 'I've given him up. He's a dirty old man. But I've met someone nice. Miss Morris, the spiritualist, introduced me to him. He's a thin elderly gentleman and he has a fish and chip shop in Brunswick Street and plenty of money.' One night this new man took me out and my mother out and we went and had a drink together to get to know each other. Well, he was just an ordinary man to me. But my mother thought there was another beautiful world shining out of his eyes and before I knew where I was she married him and he came to live at this house of hers in Droylsden with a garden at the back and a greenhouse. She hadn't been married a month when he was stricken with a duodenal ulcer so my mother had to get him into Ashton Infirmary to have it operated on. He came out of the Infirmary and he went on the back lawn on the grass after a downpour of rain to go into the greenhouse and he got his feet wet and he had to go back to bed again and there he died three months from the day they'd got married. Though he left her all his money and the fish and chip shop in Brunswick Street, his death knocked the bottom out of my mother's world. She was crying all the way to the funeral.

My young lady's name was Johanna Bertha Keim and I told my mother who was bitter and very British that she was Swiss. My mother says, 'I don't think she's Swiss. She's German, but never mind. There's good and bad in all races of people.'

Johanna left to go to Wrightington in Wigan as a nurse in a hospital. It was a TB hospital for men patients. That meant me going only at weekends to see her and I used to take her a lovely bunch of red roses every time. I went by bus. We met at a place called Dangerous Corner. I played her the Intermezzo from Mascagni's *Cavalleria Rusticana* on a piano in a pub there. She told me she was descended from Mozart. We got courting like two lovers and I used to take her out and buy her Guinness and oysters. I didn't tell her I was married-but-separated like a few thousand more people. I hadn't the nerve to tell her. I didn't want to lose her because I was very much in love with her. Sometimes we used to go to a show together. One Saturday I took her to Southport and she enjoyed it very much. She always went back in the evenings to the hospital.

Then I had a bit of trouble with my dog. My dog took hysteria. He used to run under the bed and into dark places. He used to attack me. He was a very vicious dog. I had to have him put to sleep. That upset me very much. I don't like to see a dog killed, any animal killed, I love animals so much. So, with losing the dog, I had to have somebody. I was living on my own. I sent a telegram to this girl at the hospital that she must come and live with my mother or else we were going to fall out. I went down to Wigan to meet her and what do you think I saw? On the station platform was luggage stacked about six feet high and on top was a Chinese straw hat. I'll never forget all that luggage. There were boxes, suitcases, portmanteaux. I said to her, 'What are you doing with all this?!' She said, 'I've left the hospital. Nobody knows I've gone.' She came back to Manchester and I took her to my mother's in Droylsden. My mother told her, 'I've got a nice clean new shed in the back. You can put all your luggage in there and you can come and stay with me.' So she stayed with my mother for three weeks. They slept together in a Morrison shelter in the front room. My mother said, 'She's a lovely girl. Be good to her, Sid.' I said, 'You're telling me! I've had one bad experience. I'm not going to have another one. She's genuine. She's give up her job and come to Manchester just to be with me.'

One evening my mother said to me, 'It's no good your keeping coming up here, Sid, spending money on bus fares. The best thing to do is look for a house for the two of you, an empty

79

house. There's plenty of houses to rent if you look.' I said, 'I've already seen a house 584, Stretford Road, Old Trafford, a very big house on the main road.' So my young lady and I went there to see the agent, a Mr Moore, and he showed us the house—a big front bedroom, plenty of rooms downstairs, and a garden at the back about fifty yards long and about twenty-five yards wide. From the bedroom window you could see Old Trafford football ground and the ships in Pomona Docks near Salford Bridge. You could see the bridge swing open to allow the boats come out into the ship canal—the cork boats, the weekly boats, going to Ghent, Rotterdam and Antwerp for potatoes, flowers and tomatoes.

The owner of the house was an English gentleman, Mr Kelsall. He was getting on in years. He had white hair, striped trousers, black vicuna coat and a gold watch and chain. He was living with two Spanish gentle-ladies with plenty of money. They were companions, that was all. He didn't sleep with them. He said, 'Where does your mother live?' I said, 'My mother lives in Droylsden, Greenside Lane Estate, by the cemetery.' He said, 'I'd like to see your mother before I let you have the house,' so he arranged to meet me and my young lady at my mother's house. He came to Droylsden, saw my mother, Johanna and me and says, 'The trouble is, have you got any furniture?' I told a lie. I said, 'Yes, we've plenty of furniture.' He said, 'Right. You can have the house,' and Johanna and I both jumped at it and took the house to live together at twenty-seven and six a week.

I went into the cellar and found a lovely big cellar door. I went into the back garden and got two big tree trunks and brought them in the kitchen where it was warm. We put the cellar door over the tree trunks and a big mattress over that and my khaki coat from the Territorials over that and slept together for the first time.

One day the parson asked Johanna would she like to join the ARP. I said, 'The only fire she's to watch is the one in the grate!' Then the Labour Exchange wanted her to work in a munitions factory, but when she was interviewed at the factory they said it was impossible to take her because the shells might kill her own brothers.

Ours was a gorgeous big house, seventeenth century, very old. I admit it was dirty inside but we cleaned it all up and kept buying beds and beds to let it off. We decided to let it off because otherwise it would be taken off us. In the war, houses had to be full. We furnished it with stuff from Thompson's Sale Rooms in Mosley Street near Deacon's Bank near Lewis's. The first thing we bought was a grand double bed for ourselves. It was a walnut, oh a beautiful bed. I'd never slept on a bed as nice as this. My 'wife' went out to work as a cook in a British Restaurant so we could afford eiderdowns and blankets and sheets. We got a nice settee and even an old English rocking chair. We kept that down in the kitchen by the fire. When we was ready I put cards out in the shop windows offering rooms with full board for thirty-five shillings a week.

We got a lot of Irishmen. We had a beautiful wardrobe in one room and there was three Irishmen in one big double bed and in a single bed and, when they were all out at work, Johanna went to the wardrobe and found beer bottles full of urine because they were too lazy to go upstairs to the toilet.

Another Irishman was called Pat Mallin. He had a greasy bowler hat and he worked in a bakery. He worked very very hard but he loved his pint. His wife was dead and he had thirteen children. Seven boys was in the army and six girls in the ATS, the WRACS and the Land Army. He was very proud of this. He was mentioned for it in the *Evening Chronicle*. One day I was going out of the back door into the garden when all of a sudden I thought it was raining. So I went in and I shouted, 'Anna! It's raining and the rain tastes salty!' And what do you think it was? It was Pat Mullin pissing through the window into the yard. I ran upstairs and I said, 'You dirty bugger! If you do that again you'll have to go!' He said, 'Mr Rogers, I'm very very sorry.'

One day a man come to our house with two taxis full of

81

people and he said, 'I've come from the Labour Exhange. Can you fix these men up?' I said, 'What are they?' He said, 'Poles. They're all wounded Poles.' So I said, 'Yes, I think we can. Will you come inside please.' He asked how many spare beds had we got. I said, 'Two, but my wife can get some more at the auction tomorrow.' He said, 'Get the beds and by the end of the week I'll bring you these Poles.'

The Poles come from the Resettlement Corps. They were all wounded. They belonged to General Anders' Army. They had all fought at Monte Cassino. The wounds on some of them was terrible. Yet they all went out to do war work. One showed me a wound on his back. Half his back was taken away.

When it was very quiet and all the Irishmen and all the Poles was out drinking I used to read to my wife books from the library about the sea and she was very thrilled. I used to read in real Lancashire. I'm a cross between a Lancashire terrier and a Yorkshire terrier though I was born in India. And, though I'm best at marinescapes, I painted her in oils. And I played to her on an organ. It had no footboards but it was a two-manual. I wanted a University organ with footboards and reed pipes and glass doors to cover the stops but we couldn't afford two hundred guineas. So my wife picked this one up at Thompson's Sale Rooms for about three pound. I wheeled it home on a handcart and I played it and I made it talk.

We had an Austrian gentleman, an elderly, big stout man with spectacles. His name was Dr. Walkden. He was an educated man, an intellectual, a philosopher, refined. No matter how drunk anyone was he kept his own counsel. He had a daughter called Heidi. Heidi married an Irishman. 'This is my unlucky day,' said Dr Walkden to Johanna. 'I didn't want my daughter to marry this Irishman because he never wears a collar, he never combs his hair and he's dirty. But he has to marry her because she's having a baby.'

I finished my job in the Carborundum and got a job in the Anglo-American Oil Company. I worked with a lot of women

packing 14lb tins of anti-freeze to be spread on the wings and
the bodies of fighter planes—Spitfires and Hurricanes. At the
finish I was so good at the job they put me in a laboratory. I
was a chemist. I used to go round with a little wooden rack
with test tubes in, climb on a ladder and dip them into big
copper boilers where they boiled the crude oil that made the
anti-freeze. One morning the foreman asked me would I come
up to his house for tea on Sunday and bring my wife with me.
I said, 'Yes, I don't mind.' So I went to this house on Sunday
and he made us very very welcome. He was quite a nice
Englishman but he turned round to me and he said, 'Sid, your
wife speaks broken English.' I said, 'She's come from the
Schwarzwald in Germany, the Black Forest. She's a Southern
German. One brother is a doctor and the other brother is a
Catholic priest in Lichtenau, near Baden-Baden. She came over
here before Hitler come to power. She sneaked out of Germany
and there are thousands of more people like her.'

Now on the Monday morning the foreman, the gentleman
I went to tea with on the Sunday, sent for me and said to me
when I went into the office, 'Do you like your job?' I said,
'Certainly, sir.' He says, 'You know you're working in a laboratory and you know all about refining oil and that it's all war
work?' I said, 'That's right sir. It's all for the good of England.
I'm an Englishman. It's war work and if you give me time I
can invent things. I've already invented a wheel for the Carborundum for war work, a puddle wheel. You have to shake
it instead of putting it under a press to get the air bubbles out
of the water. And I've invented a special glue for veneers to
put on wardrobe doors. They tested the glue for two weeks and
then they started using it. I never got a penny for it.' He says,
'Your wife is a German.' I said, 'Quite so, sir. Now you can't
say nothing to me because I'm living with a German.' He said,
'Are you *living* with her? I thought you was married to her!'
I said, 'No, not yet. I'm married to an Englishwoman, but
when I get the money for a divorce I'll get a divorce and marry
this girl.' He said, 'I'm sorry, I can't have you here no more

in the laboratory. You know too much. If I were you I'd say nothing, I'd leave quietly. I'll give you extra money in your wages.'

When I went home I was depressed and I said to Anna, 'I've got a confession to make to you. I've been sacked because I'm living with a German. The foreman doesn't want me on secret war work.' We wondered what to do. I suggested renting the house next door and taking more lodgers but Johanna said, 'No, I've got enough to do.' I said, 'Well, what about opening a transport café on the other side of the road at the back? We could get a wooden hut and sell teas and biscuits and make dinners instead of having lodgers.' She agreed to that but we were refused permission.

Everything was on ration at the time. We had clothing coupons. We were rationed for food. We could hardly get any meat. A meal consisted of cabbage and potatoes which we made into mashed potatoes one day and another day into chips. The Irishmen had to have potatoes, they wouldn't eat rice. One Christmas a friend sent us a big lump of steak from Ireland but it was off. My future wife gave the driver of a peanut-oil tanker two beautiful blue and white Chinese vases and he became more or less a friend to us. He knew we had a lot of boarders and that we were living by our wits' end because of the rationing and the coupons. At night he used to back his tanker up behind our house in a side yard and I arranged with him to go with a bucket and drain out some of the peanut oil, very nice for frying chips. He said, 'If there's any in you can have it, Sid. Any night that I back the tanker up just go and turn the tap at the back and take some, but don't let the police see you.' One night I went out with a bucket and I fell over a couple laying on the grass in our garden.

In the next road, Northumberland Road, was Northumberland Road Police Station and the police used to come into our house now and again for a smoke and a cup of tea and a sandwich because we had the ration books of all the people in the house. They were very kind to us till one night I crossed to a big corner gable house that had been blitzed but had a wonderful lampshade hanging in the hall, all in coloured glass. Night after night I used to dream about that lampshade. The front door was open. You could just walk in. Nobody lived there. There was broken glass and furniture all over the floors. I got an old chair and took a screwdriver and a pair of pliers with me and, as I stood up on the chair getting this lampshade down, who should walk in but a policeman. He said, 'Hello, Mr Rogers. I wouldn't do that if I were you.' 'I'm very very sorry, constable,' I said, 'but it seems a pity to leave it in this old house that's going to be demolished. We haven't got a nice lampshade like this one.' He said, 'The Law's the Law and if you take that lampshade out of here don't forget the police station's right facing the door and you're going to get me into trouble. It's stealing, you know.' I said, 'Yes, I know. I'm very very sorry. You're my friend and I listen to you first.'

Johanna went to a German doctor to get examined and the German doctor said, 'You're six months pregnant.' When we went to bed that night she said to me, 'Sid, I'm having a baby.' I said, 'You've told me that so many times I've got used to it. Have a dozen babies while you're at it!' She said, 'No. Serious. I'm pregnant.' I thought to myself, 'I'll have to get a divorce.' I didn't know she knew I was married but a so-called friend of ours, Elsie, had said to her, 'Do you know that that man you're living with is a married man?' and she said, 'Yes, he's already told me,' though I hadn't and she went to my mother and asked was it true and my mother said, 'Yes, he got married when he was twenty. Then he wandered off to sea.' But Johanna never said a word about this to me so I said, 'Darling, when I get a bit more money we'll get married. Is that all right?'

My next job was at Trafford Park where they put me shovelling thirteen tons of coal a night, naked only for a pair of trousers and a pair of clogs. I put the coal in trolleys and I'd to push these trolleys to a ramp, put the brake on and tip a ton in one engine and I'd sometimes twelve and thirteen engines a

85

night. When I came back every morning at three Johanna used to have the water ready for me with pieces of wood on the fire. The boiler was red hot. First thing I did was take my jacket off. Then I went upstairs, got undressed and went in the bathroom and there she washed all the coal off me. I was blacker than a coalminer. I did the work so good they put me in the office. I sat at a little dove-hole where the engine drivers and their mates clocked on and I gave them a tag. I sat on a stool. But I didn't like this job. There was a man there and his face didn't fit mine. He was always grumbling so he got on my nerves. He did no work at all. He was a lie-about. He started giving me orders. I said, 'No! Listen! I'm not going to take any orders from you! If you're not quiet I'm going to force your head through this pigeon-hole! I've been round the world. You haven't. I've seen more than you'll ever see if you live to be a hundred!' I gave my notice in.

I stayed at home because the baby was due. I made a beautiful cot and I cut some lovely coloured photos of elephants and giraffes out of a magazine and I stuck them on the side. The cot was pink and I made a nice canopy over the top and Johanna bought a curtain. I glued in three-eighths dowels. They was only two inches apart so the baby couldn't push his head through. Then I put a piece of string on so when the baby arrived I could lie in bed and pull the cot and rock it.

Johanna's German doctor advised her to go into a nursing home which would cost twenty-four guineas. But my mother come and said, 'Listen, lass. You have the baby at home. You've got a wonderful big bed. You've got a wonderful eiderdown and wonderful sheets and blankets and cushions and Sid's made a lovely cot for the baby. You have the baby in bed. I didn't go into a nursing home. All my children were born in bed. They only want your money.' So Johanna had the baby in bed and a nurse come round, Nurse Pontefract.

Downstairs we had a lovely Irish girl. Her name was Sally. She'd be about thirty years of age and she was feeding the Irishmen one night when I come down and I said to the Irish-

86

men, 'Mrs Rogers is having the baby soon. Don't make much noise, boys.' Sally went upstairs. At twenty minutes past twelve when the boys were playing cards Sally come running down the stairs and she said to me, 'Mr Rogers, she's had a son, a beautiful son. Eight pound it weighs.' It was on the 28th of October, 1944 and I was ever so proud. We called him Wolfgang. When he was not quite a few months old he had a bad cough. The nurse tried to cure him and she couldn't. My mother came up with a fur coat on and sat on the rocking chair by the fire. She said to Johanna, 'Listen, luv. You want to give him a drop of whisky with sugar on a spoon and that will cure him.' And it did cure him.

One day about fifteen people came to the house. They wanted a big room where they could hold meetings. I said, 'What kind of meetings? Communist meetings?' They said, 'No. We're forming a union for actors. It's going to be called Equity. Do you think you could get some chairs for us?' So Johanna said, 'Yes. If you come tomorrow there'll be all the chairs you want.' They left and my wife that same day hired between thirty-five and forty chairs and arranged them in a room for Equity. But they only turned up for one meeting. They conned my wife. They must have changed their mind and got another place. My wife had to pay for these chairs that was hired and I can only say this about Equity, they did a poor woman who was starting out in life for the money of the chairs.

We had another gentleman boarder by now and his name was Gerhart Lindner. He was a German. He was a man who took papers round for a football pool. I found out that he was a communist and one day (I'd had a few drinks) I went up to his bedroom with a .38 Colt revolver, loaded, and an apple in my hand. I said, 'Gerhart, come here a minute. I want to ask you something. Put this apple on your head and see if I can blow it off!' He said, 'Oh no, Mr Rogers! Don't kill me! You're wife is German!' I said, 'She's not my wife but she is a German and she's a better German than you! You belong to the Communist Party, don't you? You go down to the office of the Com-

87

munist Party. The girl you're going out with now, she's a communist.' So I shot a few rounds in the bedroom to show him it was a real revolver. I hit the face of a beautiful antique clock we had on the mantelpiece. The face was knocked out and stuck to the wall, and one bullet went through the floor into the rocking chair in the kitchen. I don't like communists. He run downstairs to Johanna. 'Sid,' he said, 'is going mad upstairs! He come upstairs to kill me!' I didn't go upstairs to kill him. I went upstairs to get a confession out of him whether or not he was a communist.

After that Johanna and I had a bust-up. She took the baby and went with a friend in a car to Whitley Bay. She left me with the boarding house full of people. I couldn't manage. I didn't know what to do. I was frantic. So I got a private detective, which cost me ten pound, to trace her and he traced her to Whitley Bay where she was living with this friend, a very wealthy woman who supplied theatres with sweets and ice-creams and had married a count in Rome.

I took the first train to Whitley Bay. But before I got on the train I went in Boots's Cash Chemists and bought a five shilling jar of face-cream for her to try and make the peace. As I was walking along the street where she was living in Whitley Bay with this wealthy woman I found a police car going slowly behind me, following me. They said to me, 'Where are you going to?' I said, 'I'm going to such and such a place. What's it got to do with you?' They said, 'Just a minute!' They stopped the car and took me to the police station and they searched me. They said, 'What's in this packet here?' I said, 'A jar of facecream for my wife. I've had a row with her. What are you looking for?' They said, 'Well, we got a tip off that you'd come to Whitley Bay with a loaded revolver to kill her.' I said, 'Rubbish! If I'd have come to Whitley Bay to kill my wife do you think I'd have stepped off the train and walked right to the house where she was living? No, I wouldn't have done that. I'd have done what any other criminal would have done. I'd have booked in at a hotel for two or three days under an

88

assumed name, a foreign name, and then I would have shot her. Have you found a revolver on me?' I said. They said, 'No. It's all right. You can go.'

I went to the house and I went to the back and knocked at the tradesmen's entrance. My presumed wife opened the back door and let me in. I told her there and then in the house, 'I'm not going home without you and Wolfgang.' Then I give her the facecream and when I give her the facecream she says, 'I'm packing up now. Will you wait for me?' And after tea with her friend we were taken in the car to the station and Johanna and I made it up. It's surprising what a jar of face-cream can do to a woman. I was in two minds to take her red roses but I thought they might be dead before I got to Whitley Bay. She was ever so pleased. She turned round and said to me on the train, 'I'm glad you came for me. I knew you'd come.' It was true love. To be honest, Gerhart Lindner was a German and so I was jealous of him and Johanna, my future wife, speaking German together. That's really why I took the revolver up to frighten him, that's why I fought with Johanna and that's why she went to Whitley Bay.

My last job in the North was with Duckworth and Co. (Essences) Limited, Northumberland Road. We had macerators for crushing up big beans from Australia. But we also had a big drum and my job was to connect a hosepipe to it and fill it threequarters with water. I reckon three hundred and fifty gallons would go into this big tank till it was topped. Then, afterwards, I got two big bottles of isopropyle which makes the water fizz or I put bergamot in or sometimes cumalin and I used to go and draw two buckets of acetic ether and put that in —all to make lemonade. I looked after three of these drums while they were rotating.

When the boss died we was invited to go to Bolton to the funeral. There was a widow at the reception at Dodsworth Hall afterwards. She was very very wealthy. I got friendly with her. She said, 'Are you having a good time?' I said, 'Yes, thank you.' She made many a pass. She told me I'd no need to go to work. She didn't know I was living with Johanna and we had a son and I wasn't in the mood to flirt. The foreman asked me to fill the lemonade bottles for the lads on the coach home with whisky. I thought, 'Why should it be me?' but I went round the tables. I got so much whisky into the mineral water bottles that everybody on the coach was singing. They was drunk.

I had to go into Duckworth, the new boss himself, next day. I said, 'Why have you sent for me?' He said, 'Listen to me!' he says. 'Who do you think you are?! I must tell you you're only a working chap and you've got to abide by that!' I said, 'Look, I may be only a commoner but I was made very welcome at the funeral.' 'Yes,' he said, 'and I heard about you taking all the whisky and the men getting drunk on the bus.' I said, 'I was told to do that.' He said, 'Who told you?' I said, 'I can't tell you that. You sack me first.' He was vexed because I talked to people beyond my own social standing. He says, 'Remember this. When you get in my position, then you can talk. When you're not in my position, stay as a working man.'

In the year 1949 my mother died and that was a blow to me. We went to the funeral, Johanna and I, and sat next to my eldest sister, Winnie. What amazed me was the speed that the cars went. It seemed as though they wanted to get her in the grave quick. And where do you think she got buried? In Derbyshire, right on the moors. There wasn't a house in sight. The wind was howling through the trees. When I saw the parson I was disgusted. His surplice was black. It wanted washing. I said to Johanna, 'Why does my mother have to go to Derbyshire to be buried? Why couldn't she go into the grave in Harpurhey where my father is?' The reason was that my mother got married a second time and her second husband got buried on top of his first wife, Rose, and my mother wanted to be buried on top of *him*. She didn't leave me nothing. She left everything to my youngest brother, Norman, who was then a chief petty officer in the Navy.

Now my wife kept getting letters from Germany and we were sick of drunken men coming into our seventeenth century house so she sold the house, furniture and boarders as a going concern for £200 and we went to Germany to stay with her brother, the priest, the Pfarrer, near Ulm.

Where we was living in the Pfarrer's house there was a lovely big orchard and in the orchard was cows and beautiful plums. I spent the day killing midges, no shirt on, with baskets getting the plums off the trees. Granny Keim made wonderful jam. Wolfgang, my boy, was then five years of age and he liked Germany very much. I've got photographs of him walking up the streets.

The Pfarrer took us to Karlsruhe in his car and we saw all the ruins. All the cities had been bombed like it was in England. I thought to myself, 'Man's inhumanity to man. To destroy, not to build. Why do these wars have to happen between nations, one killing the other? There's no end to these wars.'

From then on we went to Germany every year for a fourteen days' holiday. For six years I got a 'privilege ticket' from the British Railways—free on the ship and on the train because I worked in the Civil Engineering and Building Department of Eastern Section, Southern Region, Victoria Station, London. Eight times I've been to Germany. One year the Pfarrer said, 'Sid, would you like to go right to the top of the Black Forest?' I said, 'That would be very nice.' He said, 'It's cold up there. There's a lake and the water is Schnee water.' I said, 'What is Schnee water?' He said, 'It's snow water. They call "snow" Schnee in German.' So we got in the car and we climbed a long weary road right up through pine trees and past granite stones full of purple amethysts. At about a thousand feet up we saw the lake, a very big lake, with rowing boats on, the Mummelsee. You could hear men yodelling.

But the first holiday was the best. I followed a few days after Johanna and the boy and when I arrived the whole village turned out to welcome me. They said, 'Here comes the Engländer!' and they brought me everything they could—eggs, apples, flowers, jam, ham—because they loved Pfarrer Keim and because they'd never seen the Pfarrer's

91

sister for thirteen whole years. I used to borrow a bike from a man who owned a Bierhaus and go along the Rhine. The Rhine was flowing very fast, at about seven to eight knots per hour, very deep and very treacherous, full of whirlpools and conger eels. On Sundays the church bells used to ring and I laid in bed and listened to the singing and the prayers and got up for my breakfast just before everyone came out.

We stayed with Pfarrer Keim for about a month. Then we went to his brother up in Palatine. He was head doctor at an asylum for the insane like our Broadmoor. He used to recline during his moments off on the balcony of his big house. Ten yards away was his garden and across his garden was a little dirt road and miles upon miles of sloping vineyards, blue and green grapes. We could see the hospital three hundred yards away with its swimming pool for the staff. He took me through some rooms with bars on the windows. There was a man in bed—he was a murderer—and Dr Keim said to one of his porters, big strong men with white coats, 'Will you bring his violin?' and then he said, 'Sid, what would you like him to play?' and I said, 'Schubert's "Serenade".' And though he was mental and a murderer this patient played Schubert's 'Serenade' perfect with a handkerchief under his chin.

In the Ladies Wing sat near the door was a big buxom woman and she said to me, 'You're not supposed to come in here!' Then she saw Dr Keim and she said, 'Oh, Dr Keim! We've been waiting for days to see you! Where've you been?!' He said, 'I've been at home for two days because my sister and her husband have just come from England and I have to spend some time with them.' 'Oh, Dr Keim,' she says, 'I'm the Queen!' She kept saying to us in German, 'I'm the Queen! I'm the Queen!' She was a murderess. And there was another woman in there, a young woman as beautiful as you see on television. She'd killed a child, disembowelled it and run down the street with the bowels round her neck.

One day I went to have a swim with Dr Keim's son in the hospital pool and while I was getting undressed I saw a wristwatch on the side so I said, 'Come here quick! I've just found this in the cabin!' He said, 'Leave it.' I said, 'Somebody'll take it!' He said, 'No they won't, Sid. In Deutschland people don't steal like they do in England.'

It's a kind of code in Germany: 'Don't pick up other people's property'.

The South

When I come back from Germany I answered an advertisement in a newspaper to go to Hever Warren and help in a Children's Home run by Bill Phillips and his wife Anne. Hever Warren was a big house standing in its own grounds, beautiful grounds, in Kent. Bill Phillips had a beard and he appealed to me very much. He was exceptionally good with the children. He took me on and when Johanna come back from the Pfarrer's with Wolfgang she became the cook. I used to help Bill mow the lawns and he used to lend me his twelve bore shotgun to kill rabbits. All the children saw me shoot a big cock pheasant. Johanna cooked it for the staff. We had a cottage on our own about five minutes from the house. The cottage was near a wall. I kept two grey squirrels as pets—Peter and Paul. They used to drink a lot of milk and they used to bite me every time I picked them up out of the cage. I used to hang them on the wall, and on the other side of the wall was all pears growing and apples. The pears were growing along the wall like creepers.

One day while Johanna and I was cycling along the road in Kent Johanna took the outer side of the road round a corner instead of the inner side and the head gamekeeper for Lord Astor knocked her clean off the bicycle and she hurt her ribs. He stopped the car and I told him, 'You've just hurt my wife!' —I couldn't say nothing more because Johanna was on the wrong side of the road. But just because he was a gamekeeper at Hever Castle for Lord Astor he was cheeky about it and I was annoyed.

We left the Warren because cooking for forty children on the

Aga was too heavy for Johanna after her accident. We went to Bishop's Stortford, Hertfordshire, in service. A very wealthy couple. She had tea gardens in Assam and all she could do all day was sit at the bedroom window shooting wood pigeons off an oak tree. Her husband was a very arrogant man for a gentleman. I've met some gentry in my time but this man was arrogant. When he come home at six o'clock one of the gardeners took the jeep and met him at the station. He'd stutter, go in the drawing room, put on his black slippers with his name on in gold letters, then he'd ring the bell for dinner.

The woman liked me so much she made me clean the silver every day. Now in service I know you only clean the silver once a week or twice a week, but I was cleaning the silver every day till one day she opened the little hatchway when I was in the pantry cleaning the silver and she shouted, 'Rogers! Come here!' and she threw a serviette at me with a silver ring on. So I picked it up and threw it back at her and I said, 'What the devil do you think you're doing?! Do you think I'm a slave?! Don't you throw anything ever again at me, lady!' She said, 'I'll report you to my husband when he comes home!' I said, 'You can do what the devil you like!' At seven o'clock the bell rang so Johanna said to me in the kitchen, 'You'd better go in and face the music.' When I went in I just said, 'I'm leaving right now!' I didn't give him a minute to fire me. 'She threw a serviette at me with a ring! She's not a lady and you're not a gentleman!' And that very moment I took my bag and I went to Bishop's Stortford Hospital. I walked it, only about a mile away, and there I got a job as a porter.

I'd a private room with a bed. Everything was clean, immaculate, better than the place I'd left, so I was really glad that woman threw the serviette at me as I might have been there today. But when I'd been at the hospital a while they had me making beds. Now I have one horror and that is making beds, so I knew this was another job that didn't suit me—I wasn't a nanny—and while my wife went up with my son to Yorkshire, to the top of Hardcastle Craggs, to have a rest, I gave my job up, took my bag, left Bishop's Stortford and come to London.

My first job in London was at 109, Cheyne Walk, Chelsea, SW 10, and who should I find at this house but a gentleman called Mr Cecil Harmsworth King, the nephew of Lord Northcliffe.

I sent a telegram to Johanna that she'd like it here because this man was a gentleman to his shoe-tops.

I was the valet for Mr King. Johanna was the cook-house-keeper and ordered all the food and wines and beer and whisky. A Mrs Sharman came in and made the beds. Veronica was the children's nurse. I didn't have to clean the silver every day— once a week, that's all. Mr King was easy going.

Mrs King lived there as well. She was a dear lady was Mrs King, the first Mrs King, but I was amazed to see her go one day in the Rolls Royce to King's Road round the corner with a pair of shoes to be soled and heeled. She could have walked it in ten minutes. I thought, 'She's very peculiar but she's a lady.' Mrs King never said a wrong word to me or Johanna and she gave Johanna, I'm proud to say, a black leather wallet with a silver initial on it—J.

I want to say this, that Mr Cecil King is a born gentleman, a gentleman through and through. I've never met a finer man. He used to climb the stairs to his studio every night at six o'clock. When he came home in his Rolls Royce from Fleet Street he'd climb those stairs two at a time with a whisky bottle in one hand. There were twenty-five to thirty stairs and Mr King is over six foot in height and quite a heavy man. He was very energetic. He'd come down in another suit between half past seven and eight o'clock when supper was served in the dining-room. He drank a full bottle of whisky while he was dressing himself and washing himself and bathing himself but he was never drunk. You wouldn't think he'd had a glass of beer, never mind a bottle of whisky. I've never seen Mr King drunk in my life. In his bedroom he had a huge big double bed and he had a beautiful stainless steel sink to wash in, all enclosed in a beautiful big mahogany cupboard. And he had a huge big trousers-press with two big wooden screws. It was about four feet long and he had over a hundred pair of trousers in it, all laid flat on top of one another. He used to just undo the screws at each end and he'd take what pair of trousers he wanted and I'd put the trousers he left off back for him and tighten the press up. He was a very very smart man, Mr King was—always clean and civil. I got on like a house on fire with Mr King. Mr King was all right. He was a human being. I am sixty-five years of age and I still adore Mr King. I've been in service for various people, but nothing like Mr King.

He was a very very punctual man. One day he wanted his meal for one o'clock. He told me he was expecting Herbert Morrison for lunch. Mrs King had been out but had forgot to bring the chickens back for the lunch, small spring chickens. So she went out and came back again at about half past twelve and Johanna had to rush and rush to cook these chickens for one o'clock. She got the lunch ready only just after time in a steam pan and I was able to walk into the dining-room and serve it out.

At one o'clock the bell rang and I went to the door. A gentleman stood there in a black Homburg and an overcoat. He said, 'I'm Herbert Morrison.' I said, 'Would you kindly come in, sir, please,' and I ushered him into the dining-room and Mr King came into the dining-room and shook hands with him. While I was serving the buffet I heard Mr King say to Mr Morrison, 'How far have you travelled across the world, Morrison? Have you been far across the world?' and Herbert Morrison said, 'No, I haven't been very far around the world.' Mr King had been all over the world but Herbert Morrison said, 'No, I'm afraid I haven't travelled much.' Mr King used to fly round the world on business trips to Australia, America, Singapore and Japan. He was a very shrewd business man. When he was away Mrs King used to entertain all the beau monde. But she wouldn't entertain them when he come home because he never entertained any groups, only individuals that he knew personally, that he was in contact with. He didn't have barbecues, he didn't have wine-drinking.

Mr King really took this house in Cheyne Walk for the children of his niece who had got killed in an air crash. There was three children, one girl and two boys, and they were bonny children, beautiful children, well mannered. One day he asked Johanna could he take my son Wolfgang with the rest of the children in the car to the zoo and he did so. Then, come Christmas, he got a huge Christmas tree all lit up with lights and presents for the children and he invited all the staff round it. There was the nanny. There was the cleaner. There was my wife and me. He invited every one of us round the tree. Mr King, I can only say, 'God bless him!'

One day he asked me did I know anything about engineering. I said, 'Yes' and he asked me to take all the heavy old-fashioned Victorian radiators out. So I took about five radiators to pieces, cut the water off and tied them up and undone the nuts and bolts. They weighed about four hundredweight apiece and when I took them in the back-yard I did a silly thing, I stood them up against the wall instead of laying them flat, and one of the children, one of the boys, was messing with one of them and it fell on his leg and he had to go to hospital with a knee injury. I apologised to Mr King. It was my fault. I stood them up. But Mr King never said one word to me about it. He was a good man.

We left him and went to Devon. My son Wolfgang was getting quite big now and this advertisement stressed good money. I was the butler, handyman and valet for a commodore. My wife was the cook-housekeeper. When I saw this man I knew right away I wouldn't like him. He had the fishing rights for a stretch of the River Exe and I don't believe in fishing rights. I hadn't got a fishing rod so I made one out of a stick with a piece of black cotton and a bent pin on the end. I sharpened the pin sharp as a fish-hook and I dug up worms and I sat on the bridge that went across the River Exe at the back of the house and I came in one day with five spotted trout. Now the commodore he had the finest fishing gear that anybody could have. He had fishing rods and butterflies and hooks. He did fly fishing. He went up to Scotland for salmon. And when he saw these five spotted trout, some just under a pound, he were amazed when I told him how I caught them. I could see the trout in the water among the rocks. I just let my cotton down with a lead weight on and I had a feather on the end for a float and I watched the trout come to bite and the minute they bit I gave a jab and I got them and I pulled them up. After that he made my life a hell. He was bitter because every time he went out to fish with his expensive rod and his flies he come home with nothing and I caught five trout in about two hours on a bridge. Every week I had to get on my knees and scrub the bare wooden stairs to our bedroom. No oilcloth, no carpet, they had to be white. And the silver had to be done. And I'd to help in the dining-room. I was just a slave for him. His wife sat at one end of the dining-room table with pearls round her neck and big diamond rings on her and rubies and thought she was a lady, and he sat at the other end and they never spoke till they went in the lounge where there was a big white rug and a dog.

He was a miserable man—and he was brutal. He said to me one day. 'There's a wild cat round here somewhere. It's killing the chickens.' I said, 'A cat won't kill chickens. It's a fox. You're in the heart of Devon.' He had about six guns and he took the best gun in the world, a Purdey, for himself, and he gave me a twelve bore shotgun. I was frightened of the barrel bursting. We went in the orchard and there was a poor grey cat rubbing round my feet miaowing, so he said, 'Move away on one side! That's the cat!' I moved away. I had to. He was my boss. I said, 'What are you going to do?! You're not going to shoot this poor cat! The cat's hungry! It's lost!' And from fourteen feet, not fourteen yards, he opened out with the right barrel and shot the cat stone dead. I've seen tigers shot and I've seen gangsters shot, but I've never seen anything so cowardly as this. He said, 'Now go in and get the gardener's spade and bury that cat!' I went and made a nice grave for the cat and buried the cat, but I was in tears, I'm not ashamed to say I was crying. And while I buried the cat the commodore told me a story how he once fiddled ten thousand pound out of the Royal Air Force. 'You've got to be clever,' he said. 'Never mind being sentimental over a cat!' I said, 'I'm disgusted with you killing a tame cat like that at fourteen feet! What do you think I am? A grave digger?! You're not a man! You're a beast!' I rebelled against him. I'm a rebel by nature. We nearly come to blows and he sent for the ambulance and had me put in hospital because I'd threatened him.

When I got out of hospital he wouldn't let me near the house as he thought I was violent, so I used to wait in the bushes to meet Johanna and she'd come out and talk to me. I was like an outlaw. I told her I was going to London and, when I got a job and a place for her and the son, she was to come right away and leave the commodore as he and his wife were wicked people. So she passed me out my suitcase through the window and I went back to London.

I got a job in the Reform Club in Pall Mall. I was on the switchboard. When the members come through they had to sign their name and they used to ask me for mail. I seen everybody that come and go. I saw all that went on. One day a Sir came to me—I shall not mention his name because it wouldn't be fair—and he said, 'If a lady asks for me, would you send her up to my room.' The lady come about an hour after and she asked for Sir So and So. I told her where to go and she went in his room. Now this was just a friend calling and he was married to someone else. The next I saw of them they were sat on the balcony having lunch together. I didn't see the lady go home. In the morning I'd just got in and got on the switchboard and let my friend go home when the lady says to me, 'Good morning. I'm glad it's not raining.' She was leaving so she must have stayed all night in the room with this Sir.

At the Reform Club they had the biggest kitchen I've ever seen in my life and the finest French chef in London. Every night he used to cook a kind of a mutton stew for me and put curry powder in it because he knew I come from India. And after that he gave me a lovely vanilla ice-cream. And every Friday night all the French chefs in the West End used to come to the Reform Club and meet in the kitchen and all the kitchen tables were scrubbed clean white and all the fires kept low and they used to debate in French. It was like a union, a chefs' union.

When I had two days off I went for a swim in the River Exe and then waited for Johanna in the bushes facing the commodore's front door so as to bring her and my son back to London. I whistled to Johanna and the commodore heard me and said he'd put the police on me. I said, 'Do what the devil you like! I'll wait on the highway. Nobody can touch me on the highway!' and I ran onto the road. The police came and I explained I was looking for my wife and my boy and I didn't want us to split up, so they left me alone. Then Johanna and Wolfgang joined me on the highway and we went off to Germany together on a lovely holiday and when we got back we took a flat in Hampstead, what they call a one-room flat.

While we was in Hampstead I took a job as a barber and attendant in an Old People's Home in Middlesex—Percy House. They had hundreds of people there, all elderly people, men and women, well fed, well looked after. It belonged to the Middlesex County Council. It was a beautiful red building, bigger than a church. I used to do the women's hair on a Wednesday and the men's hair on a Tuesday and some I shaved twice a week. Some people when they get old they're very grumpy. One would say, 'Cut it short for me.' Another would say, 'Don't cut too much off.' Another would say, while I was having my tea-break, 'Come on, come on! What about me?' I'd say, 'Now listen! Be nice and polite! Don't be like that! Put a smile on your face!' I wouldn't let the old people bully me.

During the lunch hour I used to wheel down the ones that couldn't walk over a kind of glass bridge to a big dining-room.

I found out in the Old People's Home that the women were more able than the men because most of the women walked to the tables but the men wanted carrying about. The women sat on one side of the room and the men sat on the other. The men used to start smiling to the women and passing messages to them. The women used to always make eyes at me. I used to wear a long white coat. Some were in their eighties but they still felt about twenty years of age. They said, 'How are you going on, darling?' 'How are you going on, luv?' I used to always be polite.

I used to bath a lot of the men myself. I used to wheel them in a wheel chair, undress them and put them in the bath. Some funny words were spoken. It used to tickle me how the old people got like that. The minute they got their clothes off, the minute you put them in the bath of hot water they played with themselves, they got randy, it wasn't safe to leave the door shut. They'd grin and laugh. I'd say, 'If you can get the horn I say you can wash yourself. I'm not here for doing that. I'm here to bath you and shave you and haircut you but not to play with you. I'm a married man. I'll get myself into trouble with the matron.' It was a battle. I had to keep on washing them and by-passing where their privates were and pretending I didn't see their horns. There was another man helping me to bath them and he had the same trouble as what I had. 'Don't take no notice of them, Rodge!' he said. 'I belt them about when they get like that.' I said, 'I couldn't do it. I couldn't hurt them,' but he used to be rough.

In the end I thought, 'For four pound sixteen a week I'm not stopping here.' I was having to pay four guineas for the place in Hampstead and sixteen shillings for my bus fare. I bettered myself. I went to work for six years on British Railways, Victoria Station.

A Mr Green had a house let off as flats in Earls Court. Johanna became caretaker and housekeeper and I slept and had my food there. Wolfgang was fond of horses and used to give the milkman's horse sugar. One morning he went round with the milkman. A few days after, two burly men come to the house and said to Johanna, 'Are you Mrs Rogers?' Johanna said, 'Yes.' They said, 'Do you know your son's working on a milk round?' She said, 'Don't be ridiculous! He's not working. He just loves horses and he always feeds that horse with sugar and he asked the milkman could he go round with him. He likes to be with the horse and hold the horse while the milk-man's delivering the milk. He doesn't get a penny for it.' They said, 'Why is he not in school? We want to see his father.' So Johanna said, 'I can't get him in any school. I've tried to get him in several and there's no room. There was one school said they could have him on condition I brought a chair for him to sit on.' So the two men went to the schools locally and inquired and they found out that every word Johanna said was the truth, she couldn't get Wolfgang in a school.

Soon after this Johanna answered an advertisement and got a job as cook-housekeeper with a Mrs Hirsch in Lockeridge, Wiltshire. Her husband was a banker and a wise man because he warned us never to go back to Kent. Wolfgang went to the village school. One day my wife said, 'What did you do today in school?' 'Oh,' he said, 'they had Arithmetic and Religion.' She said, 'But what did you learn?' He said, 'About the banyan tree.' She said, 'What do you want to know about the banyan tree when you cannot read and write?!' So she went to the headmaster and he said he'd try to get him going, but all he did to get him going was give him a dog. So when she got her next job—as cook-housekeeper for a Miss Coleman in Seven-oaks in Kent—she sent him to a private school called St Thomas's where he learned to read and write. Miss Coleman was a very wealthy lady and very fond of Wolfgang and promised to leave us money. She died in 1966 worth two hundred thousand pounds and left us nothing. She gave Johanna, though, a wonderful reference to get permission from the Council in Maidstone to open a Children's Home in Kent and while we was at the home Wolfgang went to Edenbridge School and then to Germany to learn German from the Pfarrer.

After that he come back to London and went on a computer before going abroad.

Meanwhile I was living in Cambridge Street near Victoria Station at Augustine House. In the basement was a big restaurant. Mrs Elmer, the landlady, she put cornflakes and cake on the tables for the people in the morning. She used to take in men off the long distance coaches, busmen, and there was several Hungarians living there. Very nice. She charged me four pound a week. I usedn't to speak to her much, just 'Good afternoon' and 'Goodnight'. One day I came off an early shift, took my clothes off, put my pyjamas on and lay on top of the bed. At tea-time Mrs Elmer knocked on my door and walked right in. She said, 'Are you in bed already?' I said, 'Yes. I'm always tired when I'm on earlies.' She said to me, 'Come down and see "Bonanza".' I love Westerns so I said, 'That's very nice of you but I'll have to brush my hair and have a wash first.'

I got myself tidied up, took my pyjamas off, dressed and went down to see 'Bonanza.' It was just starting when she said, 'I'll make a pot of tea.' After 'Bonanza' finished and we'd drunk our tea, she brought out the family album going back fifty, sixty years. She said she had a daughter in Hungary, had I got any influence, could I bring her out to England, the communists wouldn't let her come out so could I go to the Hungarian Embassy and the British Embassy. I said I was afraid I couldn't get her out of a communist country, I hadn't got that pull. Now, on the bed was a very big doll about four feet long all dressed up in Hungarian clothes and she took the doll off the bed and stuck it on a chair in the corner while we sat on the settee. I said, 'They're very nice photographs you've shown me.' She was an elderly lady with big breasts and very stout, nice looking, with a round face, and she spoke broken English. I was thinking, 'My Johanna's not as fat.' I got up and said, 'I must go to bed because I've got to be up at five in the morning.' She said, 'It's only nine o'clock!' She'd the door locked twice. I thought, 'Why has she locked the two locks?' and it didn't dawn on me till I got in my room that she wanted sex. Now then, could you imagine me?! I had a lovely German woman. Why would I want a Hungarian for sex?! Afterwards, instead of going to bed, I came downstairs and went in the nearest public house and had a glass of beer to think it over. From then on I went in the house quietly, but every time I went in or out she'd open her door and say, 'Hello! Are you going to bed?' or 'Hello! Are you going out again?' It got on my nerves so I had to leave. I said, 'I must leave you. To be honest with you, I have a woman and I have a son—he's only a boy. I cannot get involved.'

I went to live in Winchester Street where there was an Irish lady of sixty. The house was her own house and she says, 'I'll charge you three pound a week with one meal at six o'clock. If you're not in for that meal at six o'clock, it'll be put in the oven till nine.' She was real Irish—she sat in front of the fire every night drunk on brandy and she was keeping a man of twenty-six who looked like a bum and was a ponce on her. I'd to share a room with three more men, two Irishmen and an Englishman. All I had on the bed was a sheet and I got my shirt stolen and other people lost shoes. So I went to 47, Belgrave Road, to Maria. She was Italian and her husband was a Moroccan and with him being a Moroccan they lived on cous-cous. They had two boys about fifteen years old and a little girl, and the mamma with grey hair always sat in the corner. The mamma got fond of me. They lived on the first floor and I lived in the basement and I paid Maria four pound a week for the one room with a Belling stove to do my cooking.

A lot of my work for British Railways was in the Locomotives Shed, Stewart's Lane, in Battersea, just under the bridge where all the big engines come in to be greased and oiled. I was slung on a platform on the end of a rope up inside the coal bunkers with a Kango hammer boring holes for putting bolts in. It was a dirty job. The place was full of black smoke.

I was also in the Building Department, Stewart's Lane, emptying the wagons, unloading flagstones, cement, ballast, bricks. We used to unload seven or eight wagons of bricks a day, as many as twenty thousand bricks, all kinds of bricks—South-waters, tunnel blues. We threw each other four bricks at a time. Many a time we used to trap our fingers.

It was raining one day so the foreman said, 'Come on, lads! Let's go and have some lunch!' We went in this dirty stinking little cabin with a coal stove in the corner, so I said to the fore-man, 'I think I'll build a new cabin round this.' It took me eleven months. I built a brick cabin, put window frames in, put a big asbestos stove in and a pipe for the chimney. The men used to say, 'We'll unload. You go and carry on with your building.' I made this place a home from home. Instead of the men having an hour for dinner, some of them used to have two hours. One day a man was doing some gardening in one of the nearby houses and he was throwing some vines over the railings. I put two of these vines outside the lobby with some nails and a bit of wire. Within twelve months one of them was bearing fruit. My name is Sidney Rogers. I built that lobby with the vines on the wall. It stands today and passengers can see it at Stewart's Lane where the coalmen tip the coal- and coke-lorries and the bricks are being stacked and cement's being wheeled into the cement shed. And I built the wall in front of the door to keep the place warm in winter and stop the draught blowing things off the table and the fire blowing up.

Every morning when we was on the embankment on Batter-sea Wharf we used to listen around nine for the South London train going to London Bridge from Platform 10, Victoria. In this train every morning was an elderly man, about sixty-five, making love to a woman. They used to get a two-seat carriage of their own. All the lads—there was eight of us—used to stand on a big stack of bricks twelve or thirteen feet in the air so we could see them in the carriage. The driver used to give us the thumbs up as he passed to say, 'They're on!' and we'd all shout together, 'There he is!' or 'You dirty fucker!' They were stretched out on a seat by themselves. He was on top of her making love and she was half undressed. Regular, every morn-ing. It went on for months.

When we was coming home one evening, Jim Colley, the foreman, said, 'Do you want to see a sight, Rodge?' I said, 'What is it?' He said, 'Come and have a look over Battersea Bridge. The tide's going out.' Now the tide was running about three knots and we stood in the middle of the bridge when the sluice gates were opened to let all the sewers empty and I counted over a hundred and forty French letters. I said, 'It's a disgrace. It makes you feel sick. The fish must get fat on it.' He says, 'That's every day that, Rodge. Every day I've seen it.' Bill Colley was born in Streatham and he wouldn't tell me a lie. You can stand on any bridge. You can stand on Hungerford Bridge, you can stand on Vauxhall Bridge, you can stand on Westminster Bridge and you'll see the same thing. The French letters collect up and collect up by the thousand. They all come from the toilets of Westminster. Everything is dumped in the Thames. I've been all over the world and I've never seen a dirtier river. Even the Rhine in Germany's cleaner.

Sometimes I worked on the platforms on Victoria Station filling in the holes with 'damming.' And I helped to build the three automatic lifts on Platforms 17, 16 and 15. We worked for about a year building those new lifts. They take the trolleys of parcels down under the lines and bring them up the next lift onto another platform. One day the foreman said, 'Take this rubbish to the incinerator and burn it. And, while you're there, burn the rest of the rubbish—the lazy blighters won't burn it. I'll leave you there for an hour, Sid, and afterwards come up to the canteen and we'll have a cup of tea ready for you.' Now there was a blonde girl on Victoria Station and she was very very stout and married, and when she saw me taking this rubbish round the back she got hold of a rubbish truck and says, 'Hello, Sid. I'd like to come down there with you.' We went into the pit where the incinerator was and she said, 'We'll close the door, shall we? I'll help you with the shovelling.' I said, 'You're welcome to.' When I went to get out she said, 'Don't go away! Stop here!' I said, 'What is it you want?' She said, 'Why don't you make love to me? You can do anything you want with me. I fancy you. I know I'm married but I'm like that.' I said, 'Oh! You're over-sexed, are you?' She said, 'Yes.' I said, 'Listen. Anybody can come round here and we're only twenty-five yards from the police station. If anybody comes round and catches us I'm going to get the sack and not only the sack, I might get arrested. I wouldn't do it for a gold clock!' She says, 'I've had it here before.' I said, 'You've had what?' She says, 'Sex.' I said, 'Well I don't want sex with you. Look, I know you're all right. You always smile at me when you're driving that water wagon of yours for filling the toilets, but it doesn't mean we've got to do that. You won't be offended, will you?' She says, 'No,' and I jumped out as quickly as I could. She says, 'You're scared! I love a little bit of love but you're scared!'

I remember when Royalty come down to Victoria they used to take the big mahogany doors off the room where they went in and put bronze doors on. Then they used to lay a red carpet out, bring the Household Cavalry down, put the Westminster police all round the station, and a little van come with flowers to decorate the Royal Room. When the Royalty had gone they'd take the carpet up, take the bronze doors down and put the original mahogany doors back and then there'd be a rush for the flowers. In the Royal Room there was about a hundred-weight of flowers and they were all the people thought about— porters, ticket collectors, engineers, the people in top rank— and when the Royalty had gone, the troops had gone and the police had gone, the usual routine, these men used to go in and pick some flowers and take them away to their offices; they'd pounce on the royal flowers.

One day Mr Churchill was travelling. He took the Golden Arrow, the train with the large wheels and yellow carriages. He had a suite to himself and outside his door stood a private detective. All of a sudden he bobbed his head out of the door and shouted to one of the attendants in a white coat that was going round with a tray of drinks on, 'Come here, man! Bring me a po! Bring me a po!' There was the usual toilets on the train but he was too lazy to go to them. So the attendant brought him a po. He told me about this incident and I said to him, 'What did you say?' He said, 'Nothing. But I felt like hitting him on the bloody head with it the way he talked to me!' I said, 'He *is* Winston Churchill you know when all's said and done!' He said, 'But couldn't he ask quietly and politely? I'm not a dog. He was very aggressive. I had to bring in the po, then I had to wait outside and come in for it, and I'd work to do for other passengers.'

I've never seen anything in my life so dirty as Victoria Station in London, the capital city of the world. All these little kiosks selling hot dogs with so-called mustard. People buying cups of tea out of paper cups. What's the matter with the china works? Have they gone on strike? Paper cups, plastic spoons! A man going round with a sweeper, a brush rotating, kicking up dust all over the platform and the dust going in the tea. Kiosks stuck out, greedy for grabbing money—tobacco kiosks, tea kiosks, fruit kiosks, sweet kiosks, ice-cream kiosks. Now they've got things selling milk supposed to be germ free, which I know it isn't. A railway station I went to in Basle, Switzerland, was spotlessly clean. The waiting rooms were scrubbed out every day. I went into the restaurant—at five o'clock in the morning when Johanna and I was waiting for the six o'clock train to Freiburg—and I can tell you the waitresses were very very clean and well dressed in black and white aprons. All the tables, and there was about thirty to forty tables, were all with starched linen, and the cups and saucers was china, the sugar was put in silverware. We had serviettes given to us and there was rolls on the table and Johanna and I had bacon and eggs, beautifully cooked, it couldn't be cooked better in England. We had a pot of tea (not a cup of tea—a pot), plenty of hot water was on the table in a jug and the whole meal came to eleven and six.

While Johanna was with Miss Coleman and I was on the railways, she won some money on the Football Pools, on Little-woods. She got telegrams from Titbits and the Daily Express and another newspaper wanting to know did she get the tip out of their paper. She didn't get the tip out of any paper. She used her own skill. Now from that day to this Johanna never told me how much she won, but my son told me secretly, 'Mother's won a lot of money on the Pools and that's all I can say, Dad.' Anyway, she took this big house in Kent to turn into a Children's Home and on rest days I helped her clean it over and decorated most of the rooms. It was called Stonewall Park. The parents of John Amery, the quisling, used to live there. On the balcony there was gargoyles—lions' heads and big owls. It was a colonel who owned this house. He lived with his lady in the dower lo' which had priceless pictures on the walls and priceless silver. The lady was eccentric. She used to sit in the drive and paint pictures. She thought herself a Michelangelo. I said to her one day, 'That's not painting. That's only abstract. You don't paint properly.' She gave me a big grand piano, a Broadwood check-action. She said, 'I want to give you this piano. It's over a hundred years old. If you like it you can have it.' So I said, 'Thank you very much.'

The mansion that we lived in had a giant conservatory with wattle, yellow flowers from Australia. The other flower was called camellia. We had pink camellias, white camellias and blood red camellias. But some of the glass panes in the conservatory were broke, the birds got in. So I thought, 'Well, the best thing I can do is build bird boxes, make nests for the birds.' All creatures great and small I love. I love cats, dogs, wild beasts. If you remember, animals were here before we come on this earth. We're only squatters here. This is an animal kingdom . . .

Anyway, we had forty-two rooms and the birds used to fly about in the conservatory and sometimes I used to sit and try to write and sometimes I used to play the piano, and the house was happy because we had no children. Johanna had to wait twelve months for Maidstone Council to give her permission to keep children. First they said we had to get fire extinguishers. Then they said we could make it into a house for Old People. I said, 'Never in all your life!' The roof was leaking yet the rent was five hundred pound a year and the rates were two hundred and fifty and we had to pay this out of our pocket, well, Johanna had to pay, and she spent two hundred and fifty pound for an Aga cooker. The *News of the World* and the *People* helped us. There's a photograph of Johanna sat at the end of the dining-table and me at the other and not a child in sight. At last we got our first children, six in one family and, out of that six, five wetted the bed so we had to get rubbers as Johanna had bought everything new. Then we got another ten children and by the following summer we had forty-five—five pound a week for each child. I must say the Council gave us the worst children they could find. They were not mental but they came from broken homes. Some fathers were in prison, some fathers were drunkards and one father used to sit in a chair and pee himself. Some of the antics these children done you wouldn't believe. We were never sure whether they was in bed or running about. They took their pyjamas off and fought with pillows, feathers all over the place. You'd to keep an eye on them twenty-four hours a day. They smashed things. They knocked the dogs about, kicked cats, threw bricks. They used to go down the woods and I was scared because of the deep lake there. Johanna said to one little boy, 'I'll manage you!' He says, 'You won't! My father can't and I'll do what I like!' A school bus was put on for them special from Maidstone, and Susan Cutts who lived in a little cottage near the woods with her mother and father, she used to help us. I used to say to Wolfgang, 'One day I hope you'll marry Susan. She's a lovely girl.' He said, 'She's the last girl I'll ever take. She's domineering.'

It should have been paradise. In the greenhouse we had beautiful black grapes. I believe the colonel had put down about two gallons of cow blood before we come to feed the roots. These grapes were rich and succulent. All round the mansion was blue cedars. One very very old one was reputed to be five hundred years old. We had a white cedar too and at the dower lo' the colonel had an apple tree. He brought it, the roots wrapped in newspaper, in his jacket when he was a colonel in the First World War, and it had lovely apples on it. Down in the woods there was rhododendrons that would win a prize at any exhibition. There was white lily of the valley, beautiful white magnolias, and the lake had fish in it and water snakes. I saw many a water snake slithering across the lake. It was very beautiful in the woods. There was giant big palm trees. There was yucca palms and there was the ordinary palm trees you get in the Far East. There was pheasants and peahens walking about. They used to cross our path. There was japonica and hydrangeas and there was watercress. I used to go down in my wellingtons and bring up in a basket all the watercress we wanted for the day, beautiful watercress. I used to pick the cream. Once I met some people digging. They were what they call archaeologists. They were digging for flint scrapers in the red sand. They dug about fifteen feet deep. These scrapers were made into arrowheads by the hand of man in the Cambrian period thousands of years ago when they killed an animal to wear for warmth. Some of these flints was given to me and I left them in the billiard room in a drawer in a cabinet and they're there to this day.

Johanna bought me a 1933 Rolls Royce and a secondhand Bentley, a black coupé. Wolfgang learned to drive on a tractor in Wiltshire when he was eight and Johanna was in service with Mr Hirsch, the banker. I never taught him to drive, but at Stonewall Park he used to put on my old trilby to fool the police and drive five miles to collect me at Cowden Station. He was only twelve. You could hardly see him behind the wheel. When my train pulled in I'd step off and he'd be on the platform and he'd say, 'Hello, Dad. I've brought the Rolls.' I'd say, 'Right. I'll sit in the back. You be my chauffeur.' My son could drive a Rolls and a Bentley when he was twelve years of age.

Once we held a barbecue for the children. I built it out on the paddock in front of the house with thick wire and a grid and some bricks, and Johanna bought the sausages. We invited everybody. The priest, Father O'Brien from the Catholic church came, and farmers came. A lady that lived in the big house (in every country village there's always somebody that's very rich and lives in a big house), she came. We laid on cigarettes and whisky and gin and port and cups of tea. When the party was going full swing we had about two hundred people in and out from the lounge to the barbecue on the grass. All of a sudden a van drew up and then another van, second hand vans, gate crashers, tough young men, and they all come in the kitchen where the Aga was, eating, smoking and drinking, and when they had all gone we found potted plants, wattle, geraniums, camellias, and beautiful deck chairs missing. I said, 'I'll never have another barbecue. I gave everyone a good time and they robbed me.' And after the barbecue not one of the guests invited us back for a cup of tea even. We laid on this barbecue and they were all over the house, the library, the conservatory, all over, and nobody invited us.

The people in Kent, they call Kent the Garden of England. Well, I'll tell you this, I'd never buy a house in Kent if I was a millionaire. The people in the village weaved lies about us. They were jealous because I'd a Rolls Royce and a Bentley. They didn't know it only cost Johanna two hundred pound for the two cars, both secondhand. They said we were no good because we didn't go to church. Well, we'd no chance to go to church with all these children and keeping the place clean, keeping the Aga going and every three or four hours the next meal coming up. Gossip got round that we was very independent and that Johanna and I was not married. Now how many people in this world are living together and not married?! London is different. In London you can walk with your arse hanging out of your trousers and people won't even look at you. In London people don't bother you, people mind their own business more, you're freer. If you gave me a mansion free to live in, Kent's the last county I'd ever go to. I can name three cases where farmers kicked families on the road out of cottages belonging to the farm, tied cottages. I remember my son run me down once to Cowden Station in one of my cars when I was going back to work at Victoria, and I met John Mills, the actor, on the platform. He was on Cowden Station seeing his daughter off. His daughter was going to rehearsals. I spoke to him for a few minutes. I told him he could come up and have a cup of tea any time he wanted. He had a nice farm in Cowden but from what I've heard he's left there now, he's left Kent too.

Johanna used to make all the Welfare Officers welcome to a hot dinner or a warm tea, as much tea as they could drink, but all they did was try to get information out of the children. 'Does Johanna feed you?' 'Are the beds clean?' 'When did you get bathed?' Some of the children used to lie. I advise nobody to take a Children's Home on. They asked, did we beat the children. Fancy asking children did we beat them when our own son was living with them! What these Welfare Officers brought these children was nobody's business. Toys, cheap sweets... One of them went out on the paddock and all the kids got round her and she give them all the cheap sweets going, everything to ruin the kids' teeth! And there was Johanna reminding them to get a bit of money to buy them some clothes. One woman used to come down and walk round our house seven days a week. I went out and I said, 'What's the idea coming round here every day?' 'I'm just looking at the house,' she said. She was a lady on the Council, a trouble maker, she lived in Chiddingstone, so one day I got in the car and I drove up her drive and I told her if she come round again I'd put the police on her. I told her face to face to leave us alone.

Well, our mansion had no lead on the roof and when the snow come and melted all the rooms upstairs got flooded and we couldn't stand no more of it. What with the water coming through the ceilings and the Welfare Officers coming down day and night, and some of these people not fit to be Welfare Officers we left, and Johanna and Wolfgang come to live with me at Maria's in London, 47, Belgrave Road, Victoria.

Wolfgang had a goat, a lovely white goat, called Sally. He used to put her on the table and she danced for a piece of bread.

She turned round and round and round. When we gave up Stonewall Park I found two brothers who kept a public house and they had a bowling green and a goat was just the thing to keep the grass down. They took her away in their estate car. My son was nearly in tears to see poor Sally go.

While we was still at Stonewall Park the City of Westminster Council offered me a job as toilet attendant, and for 1961 I was working on all the thirty odd day-toilets in London as a trainee. All of a sudden the Inspector called me on one side and said, 'Mr Rogers, would you like to go on night work?' I said, 'I don't mind. Anything will do so long as it's money.' He says, 'Well, go to Piccadilly tonight, will you? Have you got any wellingtons?' I said, 'Yes', and I took all my cleaning gear including a squeegee to Piccadilly, and I worked the six toilets—Piccadilly, Marble Arch, Hyde Park Corner, Leicester Square, the Cottage on Charing Cross Embankment and Covent Garden—for seven years.

I was very happy living with Maria at No 47, Belgrave Road. She never used to interfere with me and I never took anybody to my room. But I must mention one little incident. Mr Farmer, my boss at work, asked me once could I find a room for a man who was starting in the morning. I said, 'Well, I pay four pounds a week for a room with two single beds in it. I'll ask Maria, my landlady, can I take him in.' I asked Maria could he come and join me, he was going to work on the toilets. She said, 'Yes.' So he came into my room and occupied the other bed. He paid two pound and I paid two pound. He was quite a nice chap, about forty-five. Now I'm very observant of human beings and when he laid in bed in the far corner near the door behind the stove he kept looking at me while I was getting my pyjamas on. I said to him, 'What's the trouble?' 'Oh, nothing, nothing,' he said. Well, that went on for about a week. The second week I got a bus down to Belgrave Road and I came in the front door down the basement steps. I opened the door and what should I see? Behold! I see the man that I befriended naked on his bed with a queer that he'd picked up, and they were playing with one another. So I butted the queer with my head and gave him three minutes to get out. He'd thrown his raincoat and all his dirty rags on *my* bed! I said, 'This is my bed you're using! If you're not out in three minutes I'll chase you out or I'll call the police!' He tried to get his clothes on and ran out into the street half naked. He had his socks on but he was carrying his shoes and his raincoat and his jacket. When he got in the street he called me a dirty name. I run after him but he outrun me. He was younger than me. I spent that night in the Victor Hotel. I paid twenty-five shillings for the night and slept on my own. Maria cleaned my room out when I told her and gave my so-called friend notice. Not that I don't say, 'Live and let live'. Sometimes I've opened a lavatory door that's been closed for about an hour and a half and a voice says, 'Wait a minute, Rodge!' I see two queers making love, passionate love, two men, young men, nice young men, could be my son, anybody's son. So what do I do? I know they're not vicious so I just close the door and say, 'I'm very sorry. You're all right. Carry on!' and leave them to it.

I met my first queer in Queen's Park, near Queen's Park Cemetery, in Manchester. I was playing with three boys and a girl on the cannons. I went into the toilets. The doors was about a foot from the ground, they had no locks on them, and a big greasy man with a greasy waistcoat and a greasy old bowler hat on, he was about six foot two, he pushed my door open and he had his thing in his hand and he said to me, 'Can I come in there with you, boy, and you play with this?' I said, 'Get out, you dirty old man!' and I run out of the toilet and I looked for a park attendant but I couldn't find one. Next time I saw him was near the Biscuit Works in a toilet there, a lonely toilet.

He asked me again and I said, 'If you come near me I'll tell my father and I'll tell the police. Now go away and leave me alone!' He came out behind me and went a different way.

Hyde Park Corner Toilet, opposite St. George's Hospital, was noted for one thing. It was the first toilet to have glass put in the doors because I said to a Council Inspector, 'Do you want to see a sight?' He said, 'Yes.' I said, 'Come on. I'll show you something!' and I showed him two young chaps having intercourse. He says, 'Come out, you dirty pair of buggers!'

A queer will never go with a woman once he's been with a man. I say to queers, 'Haven't you got a real girl, a female?' They say, 'I don't want one. I've a man. I'm satisfied.' They used to come to me and they said, 'Pop, I'm married now.' I said, 'You married!' and they said, 'Yes! I'm married to him over there!'

One morning after night work I came up out of Marble Arch Toilet. I came up the subway, up the steps and, as I was waiting in Edgware Road for a 36 bus, a beautiful young lady came across to me. I thought she was a film star. She was beautifully dressed and well made up. She says to me, 'Hello, darling!' so I says, 'Hello!' She says, 'You don't know me, do you?' I says, 'No.' She says, 'Can you do me a favour? This so and so behind with a bowler hat and an umbrella is following me. He's followed me all the way down Edgware Road and I want to push him off. I don't fancy him some way. There's something about him I don't like.' So I said, 'Shall I tell him for you?' 'No,' she said. 'Just wait till he reaches us and he'll think I'm with you'. This well-dressed business man went by and then she said to me, 'Don't you know me?' I said 'No, but you're a lovely looking woman. Are you on the films or the Television?' 'You silly sod!' she says, 'You know me! I'm not a woman. I'm one of the men that goes down your toilets!' He had a beautiful blond wig on, high heeled shoes and a beautiful frock, pearls round his neck, a lovely ring on his finger. His fingers were slim and he had a wonderful face. He must have been about twenty years of age. He said, 'Well, I'm going down to the toilets now

118

to take these clothes off. Who's on?' I told him the name of the man. He went down and he gave him five shillings while he changed back into a suit.

Another character I knew drank a bottle of champagne every day. I'll call him Daisy. He's alive and well. If you want to see him, go to the fruit market off Berwick Street. He's broad and about fifty and wears a long grey overcoat. He sits on a corner doorway facing a high-class pork shop. When he saw me he always used to say, 'Here's my friend! Hello, Roger! How are you?' He is a hundred per cent homosexual, a fully fledged queer, sixteen stone of muscle and with a mass of hair on his shoulders and chest. He came down the Piccadilly Toilet every morning at five to five with a bottle of champagne and dressed in paper hats and fancy tissues with polka dots. He always had a purse stacked tight with silver, about five pounds worth. Instead of paying two shillings for a shave he gave me three and six. I'd say, 'Do you want some after-shave?' He'd say, 'Yes. Give me the works!' and after he'd shaved he put it under his arms and behind his ears and on his hairy chest and said, 'Oh! The girls will love me now!' He liked to sit down first in the wash room and drink his champagne and I always had to say to him, 'Look, I'll be leaving at ten to seven. My mate will be here and I want to get away. I'm tired. So hurry and get your shave so I can get my razor away.' He'd say, 'Right-o, Rodge! Anything for you. You're one of the best bloody attendants going. You're a man. You're civil, not like them other bastards!' The other attendants would say, 'Hello Daisy! Hello!' kidding him up.

Now one morning there was three policemen in the cabin with me. One was having a cup of tea and the other two was having a smoke and they were looking through the window. There's a little window in the cabin where they can look for queers. They said, 'Look at that black bugger there! I bet he's a queer. He *is* a bloody queer! Look at him looking around and he's moved from over there to there and now he's going back to there again!' 'Ah,' I said, 'that goes on twenty-four hours a day. You don't worry about queers.' Well, Daisy come to me with lather on his face and with his razor in his hand. He said in a whisper, 'Rodge, can you do me a favour? Tell them police-men to take me in on a drunk charge.' I said, 'Get away! You must be kidding!' He said, 'No. I've done it before. If one of them will wait till after I've had a shave and a wash I'll go quietly with him. I'll get a month.' I said, 'But what do you want to go to prison for?' He said, 'Look, it's coming Christmas and it's raining like hell outside and I've been out all night and what have I bloody earned? Thirty-five bob! It's the worst bloody night I've ever had! Thirty-five bob! You'd be doing me a great favour. You know what I do in prison?' I said, 'Yes, you work in the kitchen at Pentonville.' 'Yes', he said, 'and they're all queers. I'm amongst my own pals.' I said, 'I'll see what I can do.' So I spoke to the policemen. I said 'Listen, boys. Daisy's asked me something.' 'I know,' says one. 'He's asked to go inside.' I said, 'Yes. He asked me would you take him inside on a drunk charge.' 'Hullo! Two days off Christmas Day! He wants to be inside with his queers! Well, what are you doing, John? Are you taking him?' 'No, I don't want him. I'll find someone in the Underground.' They were dicing one another for him. One of them says, 'Tell him, Rodge, we'll see him another time. We're not taking him in this morning.' So I went to the washroom. I said, 'Listen. They're not taking you.' 'Very well,' he said, 'I'll do something violent.' I said, 'Don't be crazy! You must be mad!' But he got himself in that day, I believe. And that's as true as my mother lies in her grave! He *wanted* to be put inside!

Everybody knows Daisy is a queer. He tells people he's a queer. If anybody goes to him to borrow some money he says, 'Go and get it the way I get it! I have to queer for my money!' He's been in over a hundred times. I've met him coming along Coventry Street decorated up with a comical hat and a flash silk scarf and a cloth holdall bag, and if he sees a policeman he goes up to him waving his hands and dancing with his bottle of champagne and says, 'It's a free country! I'm a queer!' He makes everybody laugh and everybody knows him in Picadilly. He never caused me a pennyworth of trouble. But some men are vicious and violent. They pretend to be queers but they're dippers (pickpockets) and thieves. They stand in the stalls and if they see a well-dressed business man, no matter how old or how young, they go and stand by him and get into conversation. Next minute they both go out and the business man is buying the drinks and the other will say, 'Go on, get a bottle of whisky into you!' The business man might take him to his home if he's not married, or he might take him to a hotel. At three o'clock in the morning the dipper comes back into the toilet with the man's cigarette case, his wrist watch, and he says he's been paid ten pound besides. He's absolutely rolled the man. Some-times the man who's been rolled comes in the toilets back again. He wants a towel. He's cut up with a knife, or he might have a black eye, and he wants to bathe his face in the cold water.

I got to Piccadilly at ten to ten when I was on nights. The first thing I did was make myself a cup of tea. At all the toilets I did the same—wash the kettle out, put the kettle on, make myself a cup of tea and let my mate go home. I didn't do any work till I'd had a good cup of tea. Then I just swept the toilets out and looked for sexy books and postcards behind the seats. Every day we found packets of dirty postcards of men and women having intercourse. In a year you could find hundreds of dirty books as well—Swedish books, the real thing. Men go to bookshops. They say to the owner, 'Haven't you got something more daring?' The shopkeeper says, 'Will you come inside, please?' and takes them round the back. Sometimes these books cost as much as seven pound. I've found a seven pound book in a bag. A man's bought it and all he's done is pull his trousers down, sat on the toilet and looked at all the photographs in the book and, while he's looked at the photographs, he's masturbated himself to get the sensation of going with a woman. They generally give me a shilling or a sixpence when they go out. I've looked over the top with a pair of ladders when a man's been committing masturbation and I've had a damn good laugh to myself. I've said to a policeman, 'Get up there quietly and have a look!' 'The dirty bugger!' he said, and he banged on the door and he shouted, 'Hurry along and come out of there!'

Some of the things I've found in the toilets you wouldn't believe—suitcases full of clothes, holdalls, briefcases, empty money bags from banks, smashed up collection boxes for the blind and crippled children and the RSPCA. I've found old shoes, old underpants, in the water cisterns. I found two *revolvers* in a water cistern. They were Italian Berettas that belonged to some crook and I've an idea who they belonged to. All this had to be handed in to the police, though they don't want screwdrivers. I've got a finer set of screwdrivers today than any man in London, screwdrivers used for breaking into cars and flats. The police won't take them. One screwdriver I have is sixteen inches long. Brand new it must have cost well over two pound. But most of the other stuff I've handed in—Bow Street and West End Central. When you hand an article in you get a letter to say they've received the property and, within a month if it's not claimed, you get a card to say it's yours. I found a bicycle once outside the Cottage, a brand new lady's bicycle. She'd stolen it, rode from somewhere and left it there. It wasn't claimed. I gave it to Charlie West, one of the Council Inspectors. I've over a hundred pairs of socks (Johanna's washed them all) and a dozen pair of shoes and a dozen razors, and I've got scores and scores of lovely shirts, some my size collar, seventeen inch.

Every night I started cleaning up at one o'clock, dead on. I connected a big heavy thick hosepipe, seventy to ninety feet long, to a stand-pipe. The water pressure was full pressure, as full as a fire engine. I had to hose the floors, the passages, the alleyways, the walls, the cisterns and the bogs. Then I used Starit on the glazed stalls where the men used to urinate. I lost my smell after six months. I couldn't smell gas. I couldn't smell anything. Now I've retired I can smell as good as I did when I was twenty. In the end they did away with this Starit and tried something else. The Council was always trying something new. For the floor I used Tide because it burned the tiles. I took my own. I scattered Tide on the wet floors, got a coconut fibre brush and scrubbed them. By four o'clock I'd cleaned all the toilet. I was really sweating and, often as not, I'd to get the police in to clear out the loafers. The police would say, 'Lock the gates!' but I'd say, 'I'm not allowed to lock the gates. It's an all-night toilet.' To forget my troubles I put the kettle on and made myself another cup of tea.

If there was a blockage I used to phone up to Canal Depot, Gatliff Road, and they sent up the sewer men. It happened twice a week at Piccadilly. When they arrived they'd say, 'You again, Rodge! You haven't half got a flood in here, haven't you? Don't worry!' and they'd put their sticks up the drains and let the water run free. One night at Piccadilly the stalls and toilets was overflowing with dirty, stinking water, so I rung as usual for the sewer men. I said to the man on the switchboard, 'Mr Rogers speaking. I want the sewer men down to Piccadilly as soon as you can. There's four toilets blocked up. It's coming over the top of the seats and the stalls are blocked up as well.' He said, 'Yes, brother, I'll send them.' I said, 'My name is Mr Rogers. Don't bloody well call me "brother". I'm not a communist. I'm not your brother and I'm not your aunt neither!' He said he was very very sorry and put the receiver down. Whenever he picked up the phone again he never mentioned the word 'brother'.

Once I went near the fuse box with the hosepipe. There was a big loud BANG, and a big green flash, emerald green, the same colour as when I had my accident, cracked like fork lightning and went round the toilet. Half the men that was sat on the seats having a good crap jumped up with fright and come out with their trousers down and said, 'What the hell was that?!!' I said, 'You nearly got electrocuted, that's all!! But what about me holding the hosepipe?!!!' After that I heard one chain go after the other. They all finished what they were doing and pulled the chains and went out and looked at me daggers. I was very careful with the hose-pipe from then on. I didn't go very far up the walls.

I always had to try and wash the filthy writing and drawings off the walls with a mop and a bucket of hot water. Now, you don't have to go to Italy to see the finest artists in the world, you want to come in the toilets. The customers used to come to us every five minutes. 'Have you seen No 14 toilet?!' I'd say, 'What's wrong with it?' 'What's wrong with it! You want to wash all that off the wall. There's some terrible things wrote on the wall!' I says, '*I* can't help it! Tell the artist that's done it. Don't tell me. I've got e-bloody-nough to do without you telling *me*!'

I cannot tell what the men write because it's shocking, it wouldn't be published. Some of it's about fascists, communists, Nazis and Heil Hitler. Their language! I don't know where they get it from! And sometimes there was written with a blue or a black crayon, 'If you want a good evening out telephone so and so.' Whether the number was true or not I cannot tell. I tried to get it all off like I washed away the blood squirted all over the walls by the junkies—but it was no use trying the doors where they carved dirty names with knives.

I've been in the Ladies Toilets and the women that go in there are better artists than the men with the things they write on the wall and their dirty pictures of men showing their penises and men and women having intercourse. Sometimes the attendant's rung the bell. Nine out of ten women's toilets have a West Indian woman on which doesn't understand and is scared so they ring the bell for us to come in from the Men's. Men used to go into the Ladies, also drunken women. The attendant might be hit or told to go back to her own country and she'd ring the bell and I'd run round. Once when the bell went and I run round, the attendant told me, 'I've got a woman in there. She won't come out. She's been in here two hours.' I opened the door and said, 'Come on, luv. You've been in here long enough.' She said, 'I won't be a minute.' She had a shopping basket with a bottle of Ribena and biscuits in. She was a drug addict. She was having a fix. She had a needle in her arm. The attendant said, 'I want her out.' I said, 'No. If she's having the needle let her have it in peace. She can't be more than another ten minutes. If she hasn't gone in another quarter of an hour give me another ring and I'll get the police.' I had to go back in a quarter of an hour and I saw her sat there still with the needle in her arm. I said, 'I'm ringing the police,' and within five minutes she'd gone.

As regards the police, one Sunday morning I walked in Piccadilly. It was a quarter to seven. I was on earlies—and there was fourteen detectives, what we call the heavy squad, searching some youngsters for pot. They searched their waist-coat pockets, went down the pockets of their jeans, took their shoes off, turned them round, told them to put their arms up the wall. Hasn't the police got nothing better to do today than searching young people for pot? You can't go in the Under-ground at Piccadilly without seeing the police searching some youngsters for pot. And if they catch them they take them to court and fine them. Now where can they find the money to pay the fine? So they steal something or a girl goes on the streets to sell her body to pay the fine. After all what harm is there in smoking marijuana? They only smoke the tip of the plant which is very delicate. The only thing I'm against is heroin and cocaine.

People condemn these hippies, call them drop-outs and fall-outs. I don't run hippies down. They've got something. I've worked all my life and where am I today? Am I any better off? One MP has over fifty thousand acres of land and a castle to live in in Scotland and he has the salmon rights for a river. Now his family got these acres during the feudal wars. This property was stolen. How come there's millions like me who don't possess a brick and never will own a brick? I'm against those who want every acre for themselves and don't want other people to live. Leave the youngsters alone. If they want sex, let them have sex. The Victorians had sex, even in prison. Look at the artists and pianists of the Victorian Age! Gauguin had mistresses, didn't he? He died of syphilis in Tahiti. They were as much for sex in the Victorian period as what they are today. The only damage these people do is have illegitimate babies that will have to go into Homes. Amongst these hippies that so-called church people talk about are intellectuals. The children in this country are marvellous. I don't care whether they've got long hair or short hair. They don't believe in hypocrisy. We should be like them—think first before we do anything. Look at Twiggy. She's a darling.

I'll say this, even for the junkies, they used to come to me and say, 'Here you are, Rodge. Here's half a crown for you. Put that in your pocket.' I used to leave them alone, you see. I knew there was no cure. Several times I've gone over to a man. I've said, 'Excuse me, sir. Are you a Welfare Officer?' 'Yes, I'm a Welfare Officer. I'm talking to these addicts here.' I said, 'Look, guv, you can do nothing for them. They've been in prison half of these junkies. They've been in hospitals to be cured. One's been in hospital six months and he's been on the hard stuff again. He doesn't know if he's giving himself three grains, six grains, eight grains.' Welfare workers. It's the new thing out. These are the goody-goody fellows. They're worse than the Church people.

We've had girls coming in the Men's. I've opened the door and I've found a young girl only sixteen years of age with a young boy. They were both having the needle—heroin or cocaine, sometimes Chinese H. Chinese is a better cocaine than the English cocaine. It's more refined. Cocaine is the deadliest drug. The second deadliest is bhang. I smoked that on the way to America with John. It's an Indian drug. When you smoke it you can run into a lamp-post, you can run into a wall, with your head, and you won't feel any pain. Bhang is the Four Pillars of Wisdom. Everything comes to you when you take bhang. If I was under the influence of bhang now I could write more poetry than any poet today. You can have terrible accidents with bhang but it gives you wisdom. It's a wonderful feeling.

126

I've smoked opium. When my mother had the Plaza Dining Room on Rochdale Road, Manchester, on the next block of shops there was a Chinese laundry, Sing Sing Long's. It had been there for years and, at the back, you could always see Chinese starching and ironing the collars. My father being a commissionaire, we used to take his stiff collars there every week. I got talking to these Chinese and I got to know them as friends. One day I said to a Chinaman, 'Could I get opium to smoke here?' He said, 'You like to smoke opium?' I said, 'I'd like to try it, yes.' He said, 'Have you got any money?' I said, 'Yes, I've got some money.' So he charged me three and six and he lifted the counter up for me and I went through and I went downstairs and when I got downstairs it was like a beautiful boudoir. There was women, white women, and two white men and one Chinaman already sat up smoking opium. The Chinaman said, 'You lay down there on the floor and you smoke opium. You no tell your mother and father?' I said, 'I'll not tell nobody.' 'You no tell the police?' I said, 'No, I tell nobody. I get myself into trouble if I tell anybody, won't I?' So he gave me a pipe and he gave me like a sharp piece of wire and on the end it had a bit of brown treacle and he lit this for me and he rolled it round on the wire and he said, 'Put that in your pipe and smoke now.' It was pure brown opium.

In Liverpool there was a place called Pitt Street. This street was noted for West Indians, it was the West Indian quarter. Paradise Street was Chinatown. Now when I'd been paid off a ship, instead of coming home for the night I often went to a Chinese opium den in Paradise Street and had a smoke of Chinese opium. I'd stay there for the night and what I'd do is this. I'd go into a restaurant and when I'd finished my meal I'd say, 'You have a pipe here?' and the waiter would say, 'You've been here before? Where do you come from?' I said, 'I'm a sea-man. There's my seaman's book.' He says, 'You like to come with me?' So I went round the back with him and seen another Chinaman and he used to charge me half a crown for a smoke of the pipe but if I wanted to stay the night he used to charge me five shillings. You'd go down below. You could lay out with blankets and a pillow. And I can tell you the phantasy of opium, what opium does to you: it gives you a sensual feel, a sexy feeling. If you wanted a woman they'd put a woman in the bunk with you and she'd be having opium as well. Upstairs was this fifth rate restaurant where you had chop suey and bamboo shoots and bird's nest soup. But downstairs they'd got a woman for you, any age, and I've seen men and women smoking opium, both laying in each other's arms.

This is the only country in the world that makes out marijuana is harmful, it does this to you, it does that, it makes people violent, it makes people want to steal. A load of rubbish! Marijuana is just like drinking a cup of tea. It does you no harm. I'm taking these pills to keep me alive called Tuinal which is a hundred times more dangerous. How many people in this country die every year through sleeping tablets? So which is the more deadly?

Sometimes the other attendants used to try and shift the junkies and bully them but I always thought, 'Throw discretion to the wind, be kind to these people, talk to them civil.' They'd do anything for me but they wouldn't do anything for any other worker. Me, I could clear the toilets in less than five minutes because I used to speak quietly to them and go to them in a diplomatic way. I'd say, 'I want to sweep all these cigarette packets up and this blood on the floor has all got to be scrubbed off so will you come back about three in the morning, lads? Give us a break.' Then probably Loft or Cass would shout, 'Come on, lads! Let's all get out! Can't you see Rodge wants to clean up?!' They knew, of course, I couldn't be nasty. All I had to do was pick up the telephone and the police would be down. But they went more because I was always civil with them and treated them like human beings. Too much is made in this country about junkies. People are too fast to run somebody else down. I always say, 'If a man is down on the floor with drugs, he's as low as he can get. If you cannot help him leave him, walk by him, but don't push him further.'

Now, it's a funny thing, people say that because people are on drugs they can't have sex. Well they *can* have sex. They have it in the toilets with girls who've sneaked in after them and I've seen it. I've got over the top once and had a decko. 'Keep still for God's sake!' he was saying. 'Keep still!'

At twelve the junkies go across to Boots. When they haven't had a prescription I've seen them injecting themselves with bromide and, ten minutes after, they've been kicking the doors down, smashing the seats off the pans, having an epileptic fit. Then after about five minutes they'd fall down on the floor and go asleep. People come up to me and said, 'Aren't you going to do something with that young man?!' and I'd say, 'No, he's had bromide.' When they've had no money to get a script I've seen them screaming and I've seen other junkies go into the toilets with them to give them a fix and quieten them down. The junkies all help one another. Purple hearts I've seen handed out like bars of chocolate. They come to me many a time. 'Could you lend me a cup or a glass for a drink of water?' I've said, 'Yes, certainly,' and I've watched them throw back the purple hearts, the black bombers and the Dexedrine, throw them back in their throat and drink the water from the free hand-wash to wash them down and, ten minutes after, I've seen them staggering about the floor like drunken men who'd drunk two bottles of whisky, bits of boys of fifteen and sixteen years of age. I've seen it at Marble Arch, Hyde Park Corner, the Embankment Cottage, Piccadilly, Covent Garden and Leicester Square.

At Covent Garden there's only five washbasins, little washbasins for a free hand-wash. They wouldn't go in the washroom because they'd have to buy a towel so they used to wash their syringes and get their water at the basins. I used to tell them it was very unhygienic because this water come through copper pipes. I used to say, 'The water's not sterilised. It's only all right for washing your hands or washing your face.' A proper drug addict doesn't take a hypodermic needle in the toilet. He takes it at home. He's got a steel needle, an expensive one, and

E   129

he's got a kidney-shaped bowl to disinfect it in. But the ones I met used lavatory water and, when they were cooking heroin, they'd have it in a dessert spoon, set toilet paper on fire, boil the heroin up, put it in the syringe. Once one of them called, 'Rodge! Feel how hot this needle is!' I said, it's boiling! You've been cooking it! You're putting hot heroin in your veins! Won't it kill you?' 'No,' he said. 'It mixes with your blood and your blood's hot.' I said, 'Maybe, but you've gone down a bit lately, haven't you? You've lost about four stone.' 'Rodge,' he said, 'when you're on drugs you can't eat, and I'd sooner have drugs than food. I've not had anything to eat for three days.'

I've found a dead junkie in Piccadilly. I opened the door. I saw a man whose face looked grey and ashen. I felt him and he was stone cold. He must have been dead hours. It was pathetic to see. The police and ambulance men wrapped him in a red blanket and put him on a stretcher. A crowd gathered round till we told them to get outside—'What's the matter?', 'What's the matter?', 'What's the matter?' 'Leave us alone and go outside!' I said. I also had a dead man at Leicester Square, and a Pole at Piccadilly drunk on methylated spirits, he cut both his wrists. And I've seen a dead man on a seat. His face was like putty and his hands was all swelled up. I come on duty. I opened the toilet to see what was inside. I said, 'I'm sorry, sir,' but he just went on sitting there in a lovely sleep. I tried to shake him and I thought, 'Oh no! He's gone!' He'd been in the navy. He was forty-two years of age and he come from the country for the day. His wife was waiting upstairs in Piccadilly Circus. Some of his mates come down to find him. I said, 'Is this him?' They said, 'Yes, that's him.' 'Well,' I said, 'he's dead.'

I've seen one policeman take the junkies when they're blocked (full of heroin or cocaine) to the end toilet in Piccadilly. He used to do this regular. He used to take some poor junkie in the end toilet and, instead of helping him, he used to pummel him. But he wouldn't mark him, give him black eyes or cut him or anything. He used to use his elbows on his chest and knock him about.

He couldn't do that on me but he could do it on a junkie half unconscious with drugs! And it was not to get information but to punish them for being cheeky. I've heard him say, 'Keep your bloody mouth shut! Who are you talking to?!' I've had to say, 'That's enough. You can't get away with knocking them about. You can't do it here. You know they're full of drugs. Leave him alone and let him go. If you do it again I'm going to report you to West End Central!' He never spoke to me after that. But usually the police after being cheeked by a junkie just went away laughing and smiling. Here, at least, the police don't go running down the streets with shields and crash helmets on and battering people's heads with staves which causes concussion. Any knock on the head can turn a person into a mental case. I know because I fell on my head off that ladder in Leicester Square. No, here they hit you with their stick on the shoulder to put your arm out of action. And I can only say this. The police have been my friends. I worked with the police for years. The police have been very good to me. They've always treated me with respect. I was the first man on the Westminster City Council to ask for telephones, and in the end they fitted the six night toilets with telephones so we could phone to the police.

Peter the Piper used to come in the Cottage playing Scotch songs on his tin whistle. A policeman came in once and said, 'Carry on, Jock! Play something else!' and afterwards gave him two shillings. I was there when he gave it to him. It was one of those Highland tunes: 'Bonnie, Bonnie Scotland'. Once I gave him a pair of trousers and a pair of boots. He says, 'Thank you very much. I'll go and flog these in the park to some of my mates.' He got some money, went and had a drink of tea and a sandwich, then, while he was crossing the road in the Strand, got knocked down by a lorry and had to have a leg amputated in Charing Cross Hospital. The following night he had to have the other leg amputated and now he's dead.

I'd another tramp at the Cottage. I saw water running under a door. I got a ladder and looked over the top. A man was stark naked. He was having a bath and a shave in the toilet. He saw me. He says, 'I'll keep it nice and clean for you. Leave a mop outside the door. I'll mop up.' He was a dosser, nowhere to go, homeless. He had a little mirror hanging on the pipe where the water comes down to flush the toilet. He had this razor and he was shaving himself. There's two gallons of water in the cistern and he pulled the chain twenty-four times. After the shave he put one foot in the toilet, wet it, lathered it and washed it, pulled the chain, put the other in and did the same. He threw water on his body, pulled the chain again. Then he put his head over the toilet with the seat back and he washed his hair. The place was flooded out and the water was running down because these toilets were on the slant. After he came out of the toilet, he got the mop, mopped the floor, emptied the water into the mop bucket and as he passed my door he said, 'Thank you very much, Pop,' and put sixpence on the end of my table for me. That became a regular custom. One morning while he was having his bath two policemen walked in so I said to them, 'Do you want to see a sight?' I got the ladder. I said, 'Look over the top, but don't say a word to him. He's having a wash and shave. He's a clean tramp.' The police looked over the top and they couldn't believe it. They said, 'Aren't you going to have him out? He's naked!' I said, 'I know he's naked, but it's all right, he's doing no harm. The toilet's not being used. Besides, he cleans the toilet. He's going to mop it all up and he mops it up good. He mops it up, cleans it and gives me sixpence, all he can afford. Then he goes next door and buys a cup of tea for fourpence, and sits on the wall outside till about ten o'clock.'

When they built the toilet at Marble Arch they made a great blunder, they put seats in front of the men's toilet. I said to one of the Inspectors, 'Why did they put these seats that's here? Come and have a look outside!' He said, 'Yes, I've seen it, Rodge.' There were six or seven women all drunk, and six or seven men all drunk—on methylated spirits and VP wine. They'd buy this cheap and get a bottle of surgical spirit, put it in the VP wine, shake it well up. They used to be like wild animals on the seats out there. Standing on the doorstep I've seen a man laying on top of a woman dozens of times and having sex with them stood up in the four telephone boxes. This was with those dirty filthy women that have no home, in rags, blind drunk. One night a woman came in with an Irish gentleman. He told her to get out and wait for him outside, but she came into the toilet, went right up to the top end, pulled her skirts up and pissed all over my floor. Today they've took the seats away, and two of the boxes. The Council tries to do the best it can to keep the place clean and tidy. But they'll never do away with that sort of thing. Or junkies.

Covent Garden is very bad of a night time too because there's coffee stalls on top of the toilet steps, two coffee stalls—one where the taxi drivers all rank up, and one for the layabouts and junkies and beatniks and drunks. You never got no peace. The language from the top of the toilet steps was terrible and it was nothing to go up there and see drunken men and women having intercourse. I've seen three couples lying down where all the men are loading and unloading their vans from Devon and Cornwall and Kent with pineapples and green cabbage.

I made a lot of friends on the toilets, also a lot of enemies. When I first went on nights, I knew it was a risky job. The money wasn't very good but I was satisfied, I stuck to it. Then, as I worked my way up and was getting older, it was sickening to see the violence that was going on. I worked night toilets on my own at one time. It was me that got two men on the night toilets as well as getting telephones. Then they put safes in to keep the money because sometimes the gangs come in and ripped the old drawers out and took every bit of silver. The police do marvellous work. If it hadn't been for the police I'd have been killed long ago. I've been punched up five times. I've given men a towel and they've said they don't like the towel, it's an old towel, it's been used before, and they've jumped on me. The worst time is Saturday night if there's been a football match on. They all come down screaming and shouting.

There was an Irishman from Cork. He'd been coming down Piccadilly for ten years. One day he come down early in the morning in a bad temper. He'd been on the drink. He took me and he says, 'You hate my bloody guts, don't you?' I said, 'I hate you and I hate your guts. I've never hated a human being like I hate you. You should pay to go in the washroom to get a towel and you've never paid for a towel in your life. The only way you get towels is by frightening the other attendants into giving you one free. You've found I'm against you, I won't give you a towel. You can kill me, do what you like with me, but I'll never go with you. You've got a prison record as long as my arm. You go in the washroom and you con everybody in sight, businessmen, poor men, beggarmen, thieves, young bits of kids. You con them for two bob, three bob, and even if they give you money you smack and beat them in the face and there's blood all over the washbasins. I've had enough of you. I'll put an end to you!'

Next minute he come to my office. There's a beautiful plate glass window in the door all surrounded by figured brass. He put his fist right through the window, smashed it to smithereens and drew his fist back. Anybody else would have cut their hand to pieces. Plate glass flew all over my mate. He turned the key and right away I phoned West End Central. I said, 'Oy, send all the men you've got!' and they come down, policemen and plain clothes men, some with beards, some with moustaches. They picked him up in Jermyn Street and took him to West End Central and I was taken to West End Central to identify him. The charge room there is like a ballroom. He was surrounded by about seven detectives and I said, 'He's the geezer! I hope he goes to prison!' And he went to prison for a long stretch and he had to pay fifteen pound to the Westminster City Council.

One Sunday morning I was just finishing the floor with a squeegee after using the hosepipe. He came over to me, grabbed hold of my white coat. I said, 'Take your hands off!' He said, 'I've got a score to fix with you!' I said, 'Any time you want! Every time you come near me I won't give you a towel, I won't give you a razor! Think I'm a punch-bag? I could manage you myself only for my age. Whenever I see you in this toilet I'm going to ring the police!' and I did do. If I like a man, I don't grass. But he was different, violent. I'd seen him beat up too many men.

Marriage

When couples just live together people find out, people talk, people like the people in Kent who drove us all away from Stonewall Park. On a Thursday morning in July, 1964, I went to the court in the Strand, the Divorce Court. I went in the witness box in front of a judge and he asked me all about my wife, Irene, and how long I'd lived with this lady, Johanna from the Black Forest. He said, 'Divorce granted. Step down, Mr Rogers.' I was in and out of the court in less than five minutes. There was no alimony to pay, just ten pound for the barrister's fee and a hundred and twenty-five pound in cash to the solicitor. I'd give it twice over because Johanna's worth every penny. A few days after she said to me and Wolfgang, 'I've got a job as housekeeper a few doors up the road. We'll have the whole basement to ourselves', so we left Maria's and went to No 53, Belgrave Road with the two dogs and the Siamese. Then, three months after that, I went straight to Caxton Hall to arrange getting married and we was married on Saturday morning, the 7th of November.

I put on a black vicuna suit and I put on my trilby and we went by my son's car to Caxton Street. We took a camera with us, a German camera, a Voigtländer, and when we stepped into Caxton Hall a gentleman asked us to sit down while the names were called out. We were the first couple to be married that Saturday morning. Johanna was wearing a black frock with a black fur coat over the top and red roses. My son and his lady came as witnesses and my son was the best man. There was only the four of us.

We were called into a room with a desk. The floor was covered in big vases. I held Johanna, my bride's, hand and the Registrar said, 'Will you take this woman to be your lawful wedded wife?' I said, 'I will.' He asked Johanna would she take me and she said, 'I will.' My son put his hand in his waistcoat pocket and brought out a twenty-two carat gold wedding-ring. This I placed on my bride's finger. After the ceremony the Registrar asked us all to sign papers. Then before we went out of the room I put my hand in my pocket and fetched out a little box and in that little box was a gold sovereign I bought for four pound ten in Praed Street. The year on it was 1905, the date of my birth. I gave it to my wife and she was amazed. I said to her in front of my son and my son's fiancée, 'In case you go hungry any time, you've got the price of a meal there in gold!' She has this gold sovereign to this day and we're both legally married.

When we came home I got into my pyjamas and we opened a bottle of champagne which my wife bought at Harrods and my son went out and got some beer because I prefer a glass of beer. My sister Elsie who lives in Worsley sent us flowers by Interflora, a big bunch of roses. Five months later Wolfgang got married at Caxton Hall himself. After the honeymoon in Germany he went away to work in Australia but he's come back to England this summer to be near me. I'm ever so pleased.

Since my terrible accident in Leicester Square Toilet I've fallen in love with Johanna all over again. She stays with me all the time except when she goes shopping or to get my pills or goes upstairs to hoover the carpets and empty the bins outside the doors into a bag. I'm a lucky man I've got a good wife. The first one was bad but the second one is good. We're just one the two of us. I know plenty of women wouldn't tolerate me because I can sit in my chair for hours just smoking my pipe, thinking. She was a nurse in Wigan and now she's a nurse again. When my hair gets too long she trims it herself. She went to Smellie's and bought a pair of tailor's scissors for fourteen and six. And she's bought me a big brand new galvanized bath with a handle on each side. It's in the back and when I want a bath I take it in the kitchen and she puts some water in and I kneel down as though I'm saying my prayers while she baths me. She sits on a little stool and pours in Radox or Ranee. She washes my back and throws three or four bucketsful over my hair. She always looks out the window while I stand up and wash my legs and down below. Then while she empties the bath out I stand on a towel and wipe myself and after that I put my dressing-gown over me and dry my hair and put on coconut oil or Vaseline and brush it well before putting my soap away on the soap-rack.

Johanna does *everything* for me. She makes my bed. She does the cooking. She cooks six kinds of dishes. She can cook in French and German and she cooks Hungarian goulash and Tunisian cous-cous, she cooks Indian curry and makes Indian chappatis and Indian jalabis and she cooks good English food and makes her own jam and her own cakes. She's put my bed in the kitchen because it's warmer in there and I get the shivers quick. Slender (the Siamese) comes under the blankets with me, purring, and Nanouk (the labrador) one night and Franzel (the boxer) another lies beside me against the wall on a special old eiderdown with a cover.

Johanna lives in the past and I like her for it. *I* like old things too. I sit sometimes and I say to her, 'Do you know this furniture's talking to me because it belongs to the dead?' We've a big lamp on a mahogany pedestal. I walked into the lounge one morning and I said, 'Mamma, see that lamp? I can see children playing under it. It comes from a very happy home.' Most of our furniture belongs to dead people. She goes out to the junk shop at the corner of Tachbrook Street and Vauxhall Bridge Road and comes home with all sorts. One day it's a bed. The next it's a picture two hundred years old or a bible. She's always buying. She's like an eagle. She brought a sewing machine in the house. It must have been the first sewing machine that was ever invented. But what do you think she did? She took it back because she said it had no shuttle, and she'd no sooner put it on the counter than a man come in and said, 'Can I have a look at that?' and then, 'I'll have it.' The machine didn't need a shuttle. It was a shuttle-less machine.

She's wonderful with plants. We've a flower pot she put some cherry stones in and the cherry stones have grown. They're two inches and a half to three inches high. Just over a dozen have grown and they're very very healthy. Her fingers are green fingers. When she was working for Miss Coleman in Seven-oaks the gardener threw some stumps away of very beautiful roses. She took the stumps and she planted them and today there's beautiful roses growing on them again. In Belgrave Road if she plants anything in the summer it comes up beautiful. She handles plants like she'd handle a two-months-old baby. But what's the good? When the winter comes we've to take them inside and the fumes of the heaters kills them. We put them in the window but you don't use electric heaters and paraffin stoves in conservatories. You must have a hot water tank and pipes, you must have what they call 'humid' heat.

In the back yard up against the bedroom window we've a real garden seat which Johanna got from the junk shop. She must have paid about two pound for it. It was on this seat smoking my pipe and looking at the plants that the title for this book come to me. The plant pots are resting on wire milk-crates. When I worked at Piccadilly and Leicester Square milk-crates was thrown all over the pavements by the hooligans at night time and I used to pick a crate up sometimes in the morning and put it under the stairs of the 24 bus which stops outside our door. I used to say to the lady guard, 'I've got another milk-crate here.' She used to say, 'All right. Shove it under the stairs.' We've got about eight of them. If I go to Ireland I'll take them with me and paint them white.

I only want four acres. I don't want to own all Ireland. I'm not greedy. All my life I've heard about Ireland. I used to think all the people there were rebels and against the British Crown and I never went there for a holiday. But as I grew older I found out the Irish were not as bad as what they were painted. It took me a long time. But Paisley is making all the trouble. The only way you can get peace in Ireland is not to have the British Army there but to take Paisley out of it and put him on an island in the Indian Ocean. You've got to nip the bud while it's young. I hate violence. Sometimes I wish we was all deaf and dumb. Then there would be no quarrelling. In cabinet-making alone there's two hundred and fifty types of nuts and bolts and screws and nails. I can't name them and the finest cabinet-maker and joiner in the world can't name them. And how many tools are there? There's at least a thousand and they've all got a separate name. And every country in the world calls each of these things by a separate name. I call a nail a 'nail' because I'm English and if I go to Germany it's a different name and if I go to Turkey it's another name. But if I'm deaf and dumb I don't speak, I make a sign, and that's better than giving it a name. We can all understand that language.

I love England. But fifty-two million people is too many and it's getting more and more people are coming, I can't concentrate. You have to spend thousands of pounds for six foot of pavement to sell newspapers even. In Ireland it's different and the land is cheaper, the soil is good. I want to be free. I feel as though I've got fetters and chains round me here in London. In the country I'd be able to forget my sickness by seeing green trees and green grass and looking after my donkey and the goat and the chickens. My life's ebbing away, I'm fighting for time. Before I leave this world I want my eyes to see some beauty again, I want my eyes to see something that's natural. Here I feel as though I'm out of my proper environment. I want to get on the first ship to Ireland and when I get there I'm going to make the last years or months or weeks or days of my life the best. In Belgrave Road they've got nothing but buses and taxis and cars and people. I want to live on Mother Earth and smell the soil in my hand; I'll pick the soil up in my hand and I'll smell it and I'll throw it up in the air all over me. Then I'll do the garden, digging, turning the soil over with a pitch-fork. I'm going to plant the rarest plants and when everything grows it's for anybody to come in, no cost. I have a huge collection of seeds and I believe you can take seeds into Ireland. I've got avocado pears, apricots, melons, guavas, pepper fruit, the big black Italian peach, South African peaches and the Kenyan mango and the Indian mango. I want to have fruits that have never been grown in Ireland before, that have never been grown in England even. I'll plant a blue cedar which will grow to a thousand years old. I want this to be a garden in remembrance of me. The people can come seven days a week. They can come after they've been to church. They can come and relax in the garden. It'll be something beautiful for them although it's very small. I'm going to have some seats put round where they can do their courting or they can sit in peace and write or smoke or read a book, do whatever they want so long as they don't steal the plants, and I want the donkey to roam about for everybody to see and the manure it makes can be put at the bottom of the fruit trees.

And when I die I want to be sat down with my boots on because if you die in bed in pyjamas you know it's coming. I want Johanna to come to my side. I won't sing Hymns of Praise. I want to have a last kiss off her and to hold her hand. My soul, the minute I take my last breath, will leave my body and float up into the heavens. There are millions and millions of souls in heaven but no one can contact them. My mother table-rapped and it was all hocus-pocus. I believe, and it's not in the Bible but I believe it, that you meet your wife in heaven and you're both the same again together if you're truly in love.

I spend many an hour thinking what should be done with my body when I'm dead.

A friend of mine in Piccadilly Toilet—Big Bill Nichols, the greatest friend I ever had apart from John Ritchie—used to work in a crematorium. He said, 'You go in a nice expensive oak coffin down some rollers and there's nice brass handles and a nice plate on it and your folks are there and say goodbye to you when you're going down these rollers. But when you get behind the curtain there's two men there. They take you out of the coffin and put you in a wooden box. The oak coffin which cost a lot of money doesn't go to be burned, it goes back to the undertaker. Do you think they're going to burn brass handles and brass plates and lovely French-polished coffins?! Don't be stupid!!' he says.

My brother Tom married Ethel, the daughter of an undertaker who was called Davis—they were Welsh people—and wore a silk hat and a frock tail coat seven days a week and sat playing the mandolin and drank like a fish. Nobody's ever seen a poor undertaker yet. If you're being buried, by the time you've paid the undertaker and bought a headstone and paid for a grave—and the grave's got to be bricked in in case it might get flooded—it costs you a bomb of money.

I wouldn't like my wife and my son to *see* me buried. If they come to my funeral, that's sad. When they're going away and I've been down the hole and the parson says 'Ashes to ashes and dust to dust,' that would make them more sad, and why should I bring sadness upon living people? No. I'd like to go to Benares when I die and be burned with the Hindus. I was born in India, I'd like to go back to India. I could be flown out on an aircraft like luggage and put on the Holy Ghats and the ashes of my body chucked in the Ganges with the crocodiles and alligators. The only thing it would cost would be the fare. The burning's free of charge. But give a few paises to the Indians—or give a few rupees.

The author died on the 2nd October, 1971, in Westminster Hospital, London, SW1. He was buried in Hanwell Cemetery, W7, in a double grave. His widow and his son were chief mourners.—Editor.